THE NEW URBAN
LEADERS

THE NEW URBAN
LEADERS

Joyce A. Ladner

BROOKINGS INSTITUTION PRESS
Washington, D.C.

THE BROOKINGS INSTITUTION
1775 Massachusetts Avenue, N.W., Washington, D.C. 20036
www.brookings.edu

Library of Congress Cataloging-in-Publication data

Ladner, Joyce A.
The new urban leaders / Joyce A. Ladner.
        p.   cm.
Includes bibliographical references and index.
ISBN 0-8157-5108-7 (alk. paper)
1. Urban renewal—United States—Case studies.   2. Inner
cities—United States—Case studies.   3. Civic leaders—United States.
I. Title.
HT175 .L33 2001
362.5'52'0973091732—dc21   2001003365
                                                                                      CIP

9 8 7 6 5 4 3 2 1

The paper used in this publication meets minimum requirements of the
American National Standard for Information Sciences—Permanence of
Paper for Printed Library Materials:
ANSI Z39.48-1992.

Typeset in Sabon with Futura Condensed

Composition by R. Lynn Rivenbark
Macon, Georgia

Printed by R. R. Donnelley and Sons
Harrisonburg, Virginia

FOREWORD

This book focuses on extraordinary individuals who both recognized and embraced the responsibility to change the plight of urban America. Over the past four decades, the United States has experienced a dramatic shift in the handling of urban policies. The Civil Rights movement and the Johnson-era War on Poverty established a focused attack on the problems of the inner cities through heightened attention and government programs. This proactive momentum, however, quickly eroded under later administrations into policies that hindered progress of and even halted support for urban welfare. In the past two decades a diverse group of new urban leaders has responded to this unraveling of government support by focusing on the issues of the inner city.

In this inspirational and informative volume, Joyce Ladner, a senior fellow in the Brookings Governmental Studies program, highlights the lives and organizations of nonprofit urban leaders and the motivation behind their

---

significant transformations of American inner cities. These new urban leaders, including Robert Moses, founder of the Algebra Project, and Kent Amos, "father" of some eighty-seven at-risk youth, share their creative strategies for change and visions of a greater America. Ladner warns, however, that great leaders such as Catherine Sneed, who gardens with recently released inmates, and David Domenici, who teaches entrepreneurial skills to court-remanded youth, can neither carry on their work indefinitely nor predict the urban needs of the future. It is for this very reason that Ladner suggests youth place a high priority on civic engagement in nonprofit organizations today so they can become the urban leaders of the future.

The author wishes to thank all the urban leaders who shared their time and their stories, including those who were interviewed but were not included in the final product. The author also expresses gratitude to the W. K. Kellogg Foundation and its staff, Geraldine K. Brookins, and Gloria R. Smith for funding this project. A special thanks to Brookings Institution colleagues Paul C. Light, Thomas E. Mann, Robert E. Litan, Robert Katzmann, Gina Russo, Gary Harding, Elizabeth McAlpine, Sherra Merchant, Algene Sajery, Sarah Hobeika, Susan Stewart, Judith Light, Evelyn Taylor, and Linda Gianessi. At the Brookings Institution Press, Diane Hammond ably edited the manuscript, Carlotta Ribar proofread the pages, and Sherry Smith provided an index, Mary D. Voigt handled verification.

The views expressed here are solely those of the author and should not be ascribed to persons acknowledged above, or to the trustees, officers, or other staff members of the Brookings Institution.

Michael H. Armacost
President, Brookings Institution

Washington, D.C.
July 2001

CONTENTS

PREFACE

Few of the conditions that affect the urban poor are the result of their own conscious choices. In the case of those who are both poor *and* members of racial minority groups, housing, education, and employment opportunities are further limited by forces largely beyond their control. While some policymakers argue that poverty is no excuse, poverty is at least a partial explanation for problems that cause some black Americans to be labeled the black urban underclass. Marginalization and isolation from the nation's mainstream have systematically separated them from the societal resources, opportunities, and networks that would allow them to lift themselves from their poverty. The status of the black urban underclass has been likened to that of blacks during the era of racial segregation. The demonization of this class, resulting in disproportionate rates of incarceration for black males, has been critical in maintaining its isolation from society's mainstream.

Among those who have not written off the black urban underclass as hopeless and helpless are the new urban leaders who are the subject of this book—heads of community-based urban organizations who have exceptional leadership ability, who inspire and motivate others to become involved in the issues, and who articulate the issues in a way that resonates with the concerns of their followers. A majority of these leaders are black; a small number are white but work with black constituents. Although these leaders have varied backgrounds, training, and perspectives on the meaning of leadership, and although their expectations of what is required to get the job done are as diverse as the African American population itself, the beliefs they have in common are greater than those that separate them. They have spent a lot of time trying to figure out what works, and why. They are committed to the long-term approach to fixing problems. They are realistic; they understand that they cannot save everyone. This fortitude, this ability to not be deterred by failure, may well be the most important characteristic of these effective leaders.

This book examines the early stages of an emerging field, that of urban community development specialists. The figures discussed represent a promising type of leadership that is in the process of being defined, just as these leaders are in the process of testing workable strategies. They are presented in this analysis as the third stage of a continuum, beginning with civil rights activists and followed by leaders who honed their skills in the Great Society and antipoverty programs initiated by President Lyndon B. Johnson. The direction these new leaders take represents the fusion of leadership ideologies, styles, and strategies of the Civil Rights movement and Great Society programs.

There is not yet a critical body of theory to explain the data presented here. The field of public policy does not have definitive conceptual models on race, and studies of race largely omit the sharp public policy focus that is needed. For example, most African American national and local leaders, in both the public and private sectors, have not developed effective methods to negotiate with government officials on reducing racial disparities in such fundamental areas of human welfare as health care, education, income, and housing. This is not solely the responsibility of black leaders, who in fact have a history of focusing on human welfare issues. It is due in great measure to the lack of commitment and cooperation by the government. These leaders have done some very effective and promising work, but they would be even more effective if there were a commitment by government to develop and sustain comprehensive federal and state policies to solve the major problems of the inner city. Since a disproportionate number of inner-city residents are black, this is often perceived to be a black problem.

This is largely a descriptive study. It allows the participants to speak in their own voices about the problems they attempt to solve on a daily basis. The intent is to understand who these leaders are, what attracted them to their work, the roles they and their organizations play in shaping solutions to critical problems, and their assessments of the major pitfalls and limitations they face.[1] In-depth, focused interviews were conducted with the participants, who were selected through reputation, referrals, visibility, and informal networks. The interviews were taped and transcribed; they are augmented by secondary data.[2] The case study method is used to present and analyze the data. Participants were encouraged to talk about the challenges and pressures they face, the problem-solving methods they use, the paths their careers have followed, and the way they mentor the young people in their organizations. The intent is for readers to learn more about some of the nation's unsung heroes, who show an unusual commitment to solving the tough issues in arenas where the pay is low and the stakes are high.

THE NEW URBAN
LEADERS

CHAPTER ONE

THE LEGACY OF
THE PAST

The leaders profiled in this book are trying to fill the void created by the demise of programs arising from the Civil Rights movement and the Johnson-era War on Poverty. The Civil Rights movement offered hope and inspiration, especially to African Americans in the Deep South who were politically disfranchised and economically disadvantaged. The War on Poverty embraced a broad array of services and opportunities for the poor, including Head Start, VISTA (Volunteers in Service to America), the Neighborhood Youth Corps, the Job Corps, and college work-study programs.

When these various programs were flourishing, the populations these leaders serve had an array of programs to which they could turn for help. These national initiatives fueled the optimism of both activists and the poor, who looked to the federal government and the cities for leadership in creating programs to deal with the problems brought on by racial discrimination and poverty. Aside from welfare reform, there is at present no comprehensive government urban strategy. And although the nation has experienced the longest period of economic prosperity in history, appalling suffering persists among the very poor. While the nation celebrates positive economic indicators, the needs of vulnerable, inner-city residents have not been addressed on a national scale, and urban leaders must struggle to find ways to help these people without a federal mandate or federal programs.

The leaders described in this book could not have foreseen that most of the social programs of the 1960s and later would be temporary or would diminish long before they could significantly alleviate the problems they were designed to solve. Nor were they prepared for the emergence of new and very complex problems—the influx of drugs into poor neighborhoods and ever higher rates of violence, incarceration, school dropout, joblessness, homelessness, and teen pregnancy—while governmental intervention lessened. These leaders have thrust themselves into an arena—the inner cities—that some feel have been largely abandoned by government.

The Civil Rights Movement and the Great Society

The Civil Rights movement, which focused attention on the nation's lingering racism—and the denial to African Americans living in the Deep South of the right to vote—was the beginning of a continuum of black political participation and the backdrop against which the new urban leaders continue to try to achieve social change. The voter registration campaigns in the South led to the passage of the Voting Rights Act of 1965 and set in motion a new era of African American electoral politics nationwide. One important outcome is the high participation of African Americans in the election process. Another is the number of black elected officials at all levels of government.

The election of African Americans to the mayoralty of several northern cities symbolized a shift in the balance of political power. In 1967 Carl Stokes became the first black to be elected mayor of a major American city (Cleveland). Kenneth Gibson, who became mayor of Newark in 1970, was the first black to be elected mayor of a major eastern city. Tom Bradley was elected mayor of Los Angeles in 1973; by the time he died in 1998, he had served four terms. Marion Barry of Washington, D.C., and Coleman Young of Detroit were elected mayor of their respective cities in 1974. Harold Washington was elected mayor of Chicago in 1983. David Dinkins, elected in 1989, served two terms as mayor of New York City. Blacks have also been elected mayor in major southern cities, including Atlanta, New Orleans, Houston, Birmingham, and Jackson, Mississippi.

According to the Joint Center for Political and Economic Studies, a Washington-based think tank, in January 2000 nearly 9,000 African Americans held elected office,

a 20 percent increase since Douglas Wilder became governor of Virginia in 1989. The number of black members of Congress has increased from 24 to 39 over that period, and more than 587 black politicians hold state legislative seats, a nearly 40 percent increase. Though today there are no black governors or U.S. senators, black politicians with strong fiscal backgrounds in both New York and Oregon are preparing to run for governor. Colorado has a black lieutenant governor, and Georgia has a black attorney general.[1]

Further, Carol Moseley-Braun (D-Illinois) served one term in the U.S. Senate (1992–98), while Edward Brooke (R-Massachusetts, 1966–78) became the first elected black U.S. senator since Reconstruction.

The African Americans newly elected to leadership positions in large cities faced enormous challenges: eroding infrastructures, declining industries, rising unemployment, inadequate tax bases, failing schools, shortages of affordable housing and health care, greater demand for social services, and the exodus of the middle class to the suburbs.[2] Resources to rebuild critical institutions such as schools and affordable housing, to improve the delivery of critical services, and to create economic opportunities were in short supply. Thus leaders and constituents alike learned all too painfully that acquisition of political power in the absence of economic resources could not solve the problems of human welfare.

The nonviolent civil rights protests in the South exposed the perils of racial segregation and led President John F. Kennedy to introduce new civil rights legislation in 1963. Following Kennedy's assassination, President Lyndon B. Johnson urged the U.S. Congress to pass the Civil Rights Act of 1964, which guarantees equal protection of the law for all Americans regardless of race. Most important, civil rights was a bipartisan issue, with almost half of the votes for the 1964 act cast by Republican members of Congress.

The right to vote was far more difficult to achieve than the right to equal access to public accommodations protected by the 1964 Civil Rights Act. Voting rights protests erupted all over the Deep South and led to massive jailings and beatings and to several murders. The resistance to granting voting rights culminated in 1965 in the Selma-to-Montgomery (Alabama) march led by Martin Luther King Jr. Protesters were brutally beaten on the Edmund Pettus Bridge in Selma. The media's coverage of this event (especially television's) helped galvanize the nation around the right to vote. The Selma beatings were such a profound symbol of black disfranchisement that President Johnson quickly announced that he was sending voting rights legislation to Congress and urged its speedy passage.

Following President Johnson's election in 1964, he declared a national War on Poverty and urged the Congress to pass the Economic Opportunity Act of 1964. President Johnson was interested in a comprehensive solution to the problem of poverty—legislation that would strike at the causes, not just the consequences, of poverty. With the passage of the Economic Opportunity Act, the Great Society programs were launched nationwide. The policies and programs emphasized "maximum feasible participation," which encouraged citizen participation in the planning and implementation of programs.[3] They also promoted the view that government's role was to be that of a catalyst to assist the poor in learning to provide for their own needs, rather than assuming responsibility for the needs of the poor.

Housing and public accommodation laws significantly reduced long-standing patterns of segregation in schools, residences, offices, and public buildings. Social legislation brought about a broad range of services and benefits focused on urban ghettos, where a disproportionate number of poor African Americans lived.[4] Other programs included the Comprehensive Employment and Training Act (CETA), job training, urban renewal and Model Cities housing programs, community-based health services, the Job Corps, VISTA, and Head Start.

President Johnson also appointed two African Americans to his cabinet: Robert Weaver as secretary of the Department of Housing and Urban Development and Patricia Roberts Harris as secretary of the Department of Health, Education, and Welfare (now Health and Human Services). Thus Johnson was the first president to break the color barrier in the president's cabinet. He also made history by appointing the first African American, Thurgood Marshall, to the Supreme Court. Johnson had also appointed Marshall to be the U.S. Solicitor General.

Unfortunately, this progressive era for urban change began to decline when President Richard Nixon was elected to office in 1968. He declared an end to the War on Poverty and dismantled many Great Society programs, transferring some to other agencies. Nixon's "southern strategy" during the election campaign had promised to discontinue strong enforcement of civil rights legislation and helped him gain substantial voter support in the South. As president, Nixon shifted the focus to the creation of urban enterprise zones.

In 1967 the nation's first community development corporation, the Bedford Stuyvesant Restoration Corporation, was founded with the bipartisan support of both New York senators, Jacob K. Javits and Robert F. Kennedy. The intent of community development corporations is to make an investment in communities by developing and strengthening local businesses, investing in education, and creating affordable housing. Subsequently, community development corporations have flourished throughout the nation and have spawned a cadre of individuals with the technical skills in marketing, finance, and management. Some of the leaders profiled in this book work in community development corporations. The passage of the Community Reinvestment Act in 1977 also had a positive effect on the creation of low-income housing.

Upon his election to the presidency in 1976, Jimmy Carter—like Johnson—also racially integrated his cabinet, appointing Andrew Young to be the U.S. ambassador to the United Nations.

He also continued the practice started by President Johnson of appointing African Americans to federal judgeships.

Today, because of their bipartisan support, several Great Society programs have survived, including VISTA, Head Start, and the Job Corps. Whether the War on Poverty was successful or not is open to much speculation. Administrative costs to operate the programs became top-heavy, as a disproportionate amount of funds were spent on administrative salaries and benefits with too few resources benefiting the targeted populations. Further, competing budget priorities emerged as the nation became more deeply involved in the Vietnam War, which competed with the antipoverty programs for scarce resources. The continuing failure of the United States to win the Vietnam War was the major reason President Johnson chose not to seek reelection.

The War on Poverty and the Civil Rights movement created a national awareness of the myriad causes and consequences of poverty and disenfranchisement in America. Maximum feasible participation created an environment for community-based involvement. Citizens' awareness of their right to information that affects them and their communities, along with their greater access to education, mental health care, child welfare services, and care for the aged, is a legacy of the antipoverty programs. The racial and equity movements of today owe a debt to these earlier efforts, despite significant differences. Successor organizations and movements have developed different, more refined, approaches to solving the problems of race, inequality, and poverty, including the use of sophisticated polling data and other technologically based tools that predict how individuals will define and respond to the issues affecting them. Focus groups, for example, now an indispensable organizing tool, were not commonly used in political organizing until much later. Today's counterparts of the civil rights activists of the sixties might be labeled compassionate technocrats, as interested in problem solving as their predecessors but as likely to be lawyers or engineers who have become full-time social change agents.

Community-based civil rights organizations—including the National Association for the Advancement of Colored People (NAACP), the Southern Christian Leadership Conference (SCLC), the Student Nonviolent Coordinating Committee (SNCC), and the Congress of Racial Equality (CORE)—were effective in the sixties primarily because of their focus on developing locally based initiatives led by local people. For various and multiple reasons, the effectiveness of these organizations waned in the 1970s and the early 1980s. The SCLC lost some of its impact after King was assassinated in 1968. SNCC lost membership for several reasons: battle-weary volunteers left the movement to pursue other interests; the government made a deliberate attempt to undermine its work; white volunteers were urged to organize in white communities; and black nationalism rose within the organization, alienating white members and losing white financial support.[5] Furthermore, volunteer civil rights activists were often absorbed into social service provider organizations and permanent employment (for example, former Washington, D.C., mayor Marion Barry left full-time civil rights activity to head PRIDE, Inc., a social service agency). But the main dynamics responsible for the decline in the Civil Rights movement are the development of a conservative political climate and increasing suburbanization—a result of new opportunities blacks experienced in employment, housing, and education. A critical point is that these dynamics are also responsible for the diminished role of government in the problems of the inner city through urban social policy.

Since this early decline, some civil rights organizations have experienced a revitalization. The election of NAACP board chairs Myrlie Evers-Williams in 1995 and Julian Bond in 1998 give added respectability to the oldest civil rights organization in America. Under the leadership of its president, former U.S. congressman Kwesi Mfume, the NAACP is tackling such issues as discrimination in television programming and corporate hiring of blacks. In 2000 the organization launched a massive get-out-the-vote campaign for the presidential election.[6] Under the leadership of Hugh Price, the National Urban League has also crafted a new agenda, focusing on the digital divide, urban schools, and the recurring issues of employment and training.[7]

Falling through the Safety Net

President Ronald Reagan's urban policies of the 1980s redefined the problems of the inner cities. Funding for urban policy initiatives was cut, and a generally hostile attitude toward civil rights and social welfare prevailed. The Reagan administration's policies and actions on race were symbolically exemplified by the president's refusal to meet with black elected officials who wished to lay before him the critical issues of their constituents; by his use of the term "welfare queen" to imply that most or all welfare recipients abused the system; and by his campaign visit to Philadelphia, Mississippi, where three civil rights workers were brutally murdered in the summer of 1964.

As public resources for urban reform were depleted, so were private resources, as the commercial and housing industries withdrew from urban centers to concentrate their expansion into suburbia. Billions of dollars were diverted from urban social programs in this way. Since there are large concentrations of blacks in the inner cities, they were the group most affected. Programs that promote their uplift and that were part of the earlier urban strategy were eliminated.

Adding to the problem was the industrial shift beginning in earnest in the 1970s, as manufacturers moved from the major cities of the North to the Sun Belt and to offshore locations. The good jobs, upon which generations of African Americans relied to become upwardly mobile, have declined and have rarely been replaced with comparable opportunities. Blacks who prospered in the automotive industry, for example, find few opportunities with comparable compensation in the service industries. A bifurcation has emerged in the service sector, with a demand for both very low-skilled and very high-skilled labor. Jobs that fit the industrial work skills of newly unemployed blacks are notably absent, as are publicly funded job training programs for displaced workers. Another factor affecting the employment picture is the changing demographics, as new immigrants take jobs in fields once dominated by African Americans.[8]

As legitimate avenues to upward mobility are restricted, the drug economy flourishes, further weakening working-class black families and their neighborhoods. Drug sales have brought a highly profitable underground economy to these neighborhoods even as it causes the most heinous destruction. The combination of poverty, drugs, and violence has created an unprecedented and destructive dynamic in once-stable communities. The drug culture has an impact on every aspect of the health and welfare of low-income and working-class black families and communities, from an increase in maternal drug addiction to an increase in the incarceration of minors. The spiral of poverty reaches across generations, as the erosion of traditional values and the legitimate opportunity structure leaves in its wake even less optimism about the future.[9]

Although community activists were able to mobilize around a southern civil rights strategy, they could not as easily identify the priorities in northern cities, nor was it as simple to know what to do about them. It is more difficult to solve the tough human welfare problems of drug addiction, incarceration, and chronic unemployment than to register disfranchised people to vote or to provide equal access to restaurants and other public facilities. As the activists floundered, other groups, seizing the opportunities offered by the state, legitimized their issues and needs. Walter Stafford, author of *Black Civil Society in New York City*, says, "We did not develop a strategy for the way in which states distributed power and dealt with constituent interests of poor minorities. Now we are looking for a strategy that bubbles up from the voluntary sector that can inform elected officials on how best to execute many of their functions."[10]

The support network for the poor thus diminished at a time when it was needed most. The shift in paradigms under the Reagan presidency, from government accepting responsibility for the poor to a model of volunteerism, has redefined the parameters of responsibility for the welfare of citizens. The first line of defense is no longer government but the individual, the family, and civil society. President George Bush continued the policy orientation of President Reagan; his "thousand points of light" gave a name to volunteerism in his administration.

The work of the new urban leaders profiled in this book is to define the new civil rights agenda in light of the paradigm shift—to clarify the critical issues and to resolve them with the resources at hand in an era when government support for change has greatly diminished. The need is substantial, and the means to meet these needs are scarce. The new urban leaders are, as political scientist Ronald Walters says, "trying to spin gold from straw."[11]

PART ONE

ON BECOMING A
NEW URBAN LEADER

CHAPTER TWO

KENT AMOS

Our task is to transform rundown neighborhoods into revitalized neighborhoods. We have new windows where boards used to be. We have new fencing where no fencing used to be. We have paint where peeling used to be. We have clean walls where graffiti used to be. . . . We have hope where despair used to be. We have dreams where nightmares used to be. We have children engaged with adults where children used to scare adults. We have generational involvement. All of that can come together by having belief in one another as fellow human beings.

—KENT AMOS

Kent Amos left an executive position at the Xerox Corporation to become a surrogate parent (although he is quick to say that these are his "real" children), mentor, service provider, and advocate to more than eighty chil-

15

dren growing up in the inner city of Washington, D.C.[1] His work has been featured in major publications, including a cover story in *Parade Magazine* in May 1987. He founded the Urban Family Institute in 1991 as a nonprofit community development organization, dedicated to supporting families and creating a seamless web of care for children. His goal is to do,

Kent Amos

on a broad scale, the same kind of mentoring he did informally for a decade in his own home.

Amos is a fourth-generation Washingtonian and a product of the D.C. public school system during a time when schools such as Dunbar were excellent. His mother taught in the public school system for thirty-two years; his father, who graduated from Dunbar High School, was a lawyer. His grandfather and grandmother met while she was a senior and he was a first-year teacher at Armstrong High School. His grandfather taught music for forty-seven years at Dunbar and Armstrong High Schools, a career further distinguished by the fact that Duke Ellington was among his music students. The charter school that the Urban Family Institute opened in the old Armstrong High School building—the Benjamin and Gladys Amos Campus—bears his grandparents' name.

Amos's career as a leader in addressing the problems of inner-city children began when Amos and his wife, Carmen, were confronted with the question of where to send their own two children to school. Given how well the public schools had prepared him, Amos wondered, "Why shouldn't I put my kids in D.C. public schools?" And to the consternation of many of their middle-class friends whose children were in private schools, the Amoses did enroll their children in public school. Amos says, "I believe the reason why the public system, nationally, is [so poor] is because the people who have resources abandon them. And I was not going to do that." Doing "that" would also have changed life's course—for him, especially, and also for his family.

Amos's involvement began in 1982, when the eldest Amos son, Wesley, was considering attending Coolidge High School, the school from which Amos graduated. Frank Williams, who had been Amos's classmate at Coolidge and was now the school's boys' basketball coach, encouraged Amos to enroll Wesley, promising, "I'll take care of your son if you give him a chance to come."

During the summer before enrolling in school, Wesley played summer league basketball at Coolidge. He spoke frequently of his newfound friends, Milton "T-bone" and Daryl. When these boys walked into his house, Amos remembers saying, "Oh my gracious, we have a problem here," but rather than running from the problem, "I ran toward . . . it." He invited the boys into their home, got to know them, and worked to help them change. By intervening in the boys' lives, "we really were intervening in our child's life as well. That was the purpose." To save their son, "we had to save his friends." By the end of the summer, Daryl and Milton T-bone had recruited seven of their friends into the group that met at the Amos house.

Amos took the initiative to meet the boys' parents, who agreed to allow the Amoses to set the rules for their sons if the Amoses supplied the resources. The Amoses set rules and schedules. The children had to do their homework, study for examinations, pass their courses, and stay out of trouble. Amos visited their teachers to check on their progress. He was a strong disciplinarian, and the children respected him. He asked all of them to call him Dad, not distinguishing between them and his own kids. The children were free to come to the Amos home at any time and were encouraged to bring a friend. Slowly, they began to avoid street life and its dangers. Amos was successful in getting children who never dreamed even of finishing high school into college. He attended all of their graduations, and his involvement with them continues. He bears the pride of a father realizing the fruit of his labor.

After operating the after-school program in their home on an informal basis for a few years, Kent Amos left his job at Xerox to devote all of his time to what had become his mission in life: to save at-risk, black, inner-city children from the dangers of the streets by helping them complete high school and college. In addition to the $600,000 of his own funds that he spent, he received another $400,000 from the Xerox Corporation. Along the way, he mortgaged the family home and fought off two foreclosures; each time, friends and supporters came to his aid. By the time the Amos daughter, Debra, who is younger than their son, was in high school, most of the children in their home were girls, because she did the recruiting. Over the eleven years of their efforts, some eighty-seven children were brought into their home. It was a very costly endeavor, Amos says. "I took all of our life savings and all my retirement money from Xerox." Obviously, the returns on the investment were worth it. "Seventy-three kids have gone to college, sixty-one have graduated from college, and fourteen have advanced degrees," Amos recounts.

Perhaps the greatest transformation, however, is Amos's. His mentoring role was only the beginning. Amos is now recognized as a national advocate for children and families in poor urban communities. Amos credits his training in military combat in Vietnam and his experiences in business for his ability to take such high risks in pursuing his vision of changing the lives of children at greatest risk. What motivates him and drives his mission is his deep personal conviction that all children deserve to have a chance to succeed.

"If you ask me if I'm a true believer, the answer to that is absolutely, unequivocally yes. You want to know why I now do what I do?" he asks. "Because five of them [his informally adopted sons] have been murdered. I had three boys shot to death, one boy stabbed, and one boy hung." When asked if he could have predicted which ones would have succeeded, he responds,

> No—well, one—not really. There were no signs that made me think that I couldn't save any of them. It wasn't that kind of deal. The first boy to die, William Andre Jackson, was a drug dealer when he came to us. The rule in our house was that any kid could bring home any other kid any time for any reason. David brought Andre home with him. David said to me before he came home, in spite of the rule, "Dad, you've got to understand, Andre is a gun-toting drug dealer." I said, "Fine, bring him home." The child was my son's buddy, neighbor, and his childhood friend. I said, "Bring him anyway." He said, "I believe this world [the Amos home] can help him." And I said "That's right."

When Andre came to his house, Amos took him into the library, shut the door, and said, "This is the deal, son. We do things as a family. We study, we learn, we eat dinner together, and we go to bed as a family. He never mentioned the gun; he never mentioned the drugs. He reluctantly bought into the process. In almost a year, he became a good student, and he was great around the house. He was a wonderful kid."

However, the problems this young man tried to leave behind eventually caught up with him. He came to Amos eight or nine months later, told him he had a problem, and handed him a gun, telling him that he was involved in a homicide. Amos asked, "You killed somebody?" Andre said, "No. The guy I worked for did. On a collection [for a drug debt]. And this is the gun. He gave me the gun. So now I'm involved in this homicide." Amos said, "Yeah, you are."

Amos took Andre to District of Columbia police chief Maurice Turner, who sought counsel from the city's Corporation Counsel and the U.S. Attorney's Office. In the end, Andre had to testify. He was willing to go to jail, and Amos says that Andre felt good about this decision. However, Andre was murdered before the trial by the boy he was going to testify against. Andre was the first of Amos's children to die.

Amos goes down the list as he talks about the other four who died. One boy was hung by other boys on his sixteenth birthday because he refused to sell drugs. He was planning to bring a number of other boys to the Amos safe haven, but drug dealers, who did not want that to happen, intervened and killed him. The third boy was a student at Northeastern University in Boston. During a basketball game on an outdoor court, he got into an argument with a fourteen-year-old boy over a basketball. The boy went home, got a butcher knife, and came back and stabbed the young man in the back while he was playing. The fourth boy, a student at Norfolk (Virginia) State University, was gunned down in front of a 7-11 store. Amos believes that this boy was involved in drug trafficking. "I don't believe it was random," he says somberly.

The most senseless of the murders was so recent that Amos shakes his head as he talks about the agony that replaced so much promise. This young man was a twenty-eight-year-old college graduate, very nice, hard working. He was at his girlfriend's house when a man called and started an argument with her. Amos's son took the telephone from her and argued with the caller. As he was leaving the house, the caller appeared and shot him in the back of the head.

In Kent Amos's work, there is no way to predict who is going to live or who is going to die, when even a college graduate is still highly at risk to lose his life over something senseless.

For the most part, the killings were random. Some of these young people appear never to completely get away from violence, because it is so widespread and because they grew up in it. What is unusual is that the murders have not defeated Amos or made him cynical; they have given him a renewed sense of purpose—a mission, he calls it. He knows that no matter how much investment he makes in the children and families he works with, it can be undermined by destructive forces for whom life means little to nothing. As he talks to audiences across the country about violence, he reminds them of the deaths of children. "Nine children are murdered by homicide, two by suicide, and two by accident every single day." He wants to end the senseless killing and end the pain they leave behind—for his family and for other families.[2]

At first glance, there is little in Amos's background that would have caused others to envision him in his current role. He is a third-generation college graduate and has been a combat officer in Vietnam and a vice president of one of the nation's largest corporations. Amos is careful to emphasize that he is the "recipient of the opportunity to use my skills to the fullest in corporate America" and that this was "made possible by those who came before me." He says that "affirmative action was the codifying of those sacrifices by others."[3] But he has used his military leadership skills and his corporate leadership skills to enter another area, which he has taken to the level of high stakes. Few individuals would have had the courage to bring into their middle-class home children who were drug dealers and involved in other deviant and illegal behavior. But Amos was motivated by the challenge itself:

You don't walk away from a Fortune 500 vice presidency to run a small nonprofit organization for economic gain.

The reason you do it is because you want to do something different. Einstein tells us that the significant problems we face today cannot be solved by the same kind of thinking that led to the problems in the first place. Therefore, you have to think differently. So we're in the business of thinking and acting differently. So what did we do? We said, Okay, what is the problem? The problem is a developmental one. What's happened in Littleton, Colorado [the killings at Columbine High School], and . . . all around this country, is a function of development. No one is born to [be violent]. These are a function of what a child learns in his culture and environment.

Amos is attempting to create smaller villages within the cities in which he has established Urban Family Institutes. In Washington, D.C., participating children come from nine public housing sites. There the institute offers parent training classes three times a week; two centers offer adult training. There are Kids Houses (see below) in fourteen states; fourteen schools are in operation throughout the country. To achieve these ends, the Urban Family Institute formed a partnership with Community Academy, a school management organization, to create the Learn Now Community Academy. The academy's goal is to enable families to become healthy, stable, and independent—and committed to staying in their old communities and rebuilding them instead of fleeing to the suburbs. Amos worries that the problems of the inner city cannot be resolved without population stability. He also emphasizes that playgrounds are central to the health and welfare of these communities, that they must be controlled by the community and, in some cases, taken back from the drug dealers.

Much of Amos's program is focused on children's psycho-social developmental needs. The program called Kids House gives adults an opportunity to create safe and caring places where children can go when they are not in school. These adults, preferably from the neighborhoods where the programs are located, are recruited and trained to work as volunteer leaders. They use the Kurriculum Integrated Development System (KIDS) to teach children in Kids Houses in Washington, New Orleans, Los Angeles, Chicago, Chattanooga, Lakeland, Florida, Wichita, Kansas, and Salinas, California.[4] A site is also located at the Eastern Correctional Institution in Princess Anne County, Maryland, where male inmates are taught parenting skills that help them to interact with their children when they come to visit. The purpose is to also help them to be good parents and remain involved in their children's lives when they are released from prison. To date, six classes have graduated from the program.

At Kids House, children and adults do homework, read, play, talk, share a family-style meal, and become, in effect, an extended family. It is an extension of the safe haven that Amos and his wife provided, where they functioned as parents when the biological parents could not or would not.

Other Urban Family Institute programs are designed to revitalize neighborhoods in the Shaw and Petworth sections of the District of Columbia. Some of the institute's work is done in collaboration with city government agencies, such as the public schools, where it works to establish charter schools. It also works with the recreation department, which controls the playgrounds, and public housing authorities, who control public housing, where some Kids Houses are located.

"Kids House also got us into the public housing arena, where we discovered that the adults in that community needed support as well," Amos says. He feels that many poor, troubled people—like some of those he works with in public housing—have not managed to negotiate the public and private systems they encounter. If they had done so, they would not be in public housing. On a tour of one of the public housing projects where a Kids House is located, Amos introduced me to several female staff members whose lives have been transformed as a result of their work with Amos's program. One woman hired to work in the Kids House program—a former IV drug user who has the AIDS virus—discovered a sense of purpose and hope in her new work. She stopped using drugs, supported Amos in getting the drug dealers out of the housing project, and began a new career as a teacher in the after-school program in the housing project. She uses her skills to help the children, her own included, with their homework and other after-school activities.

Amos's chance encounter with troubled boys—when his son brought his friends home that fateful day—could have ended with Amos demanding that his son not invite them home again because they were from different social backgrounds and would have a negative influence on his son. However, Amos's predisposition is to face challenges instead of avoiding them, and he saw an opportunity to save young lives rather than cast them back into the streets. He was also deeply influenced by the fact that he comes from a family of educators and that he saw combat in Vietnam. Both influenced him to take an unorthodox approach to solving the problems of at-risk urban children and their families. Amos is aware of how far he might have advanced had he stayed with the Xerox Corporation, but he has no regrets. And although friends have suggested that he take a corporate job that would offer him and his wife financial security, his stronger sense is that he has a mission, and nothing can deter him.

However, the real issue is whether Amos can translate the successes he had with his informally adopted children to the thousands of children in the programs he has established in several cities. Is it possible to train young leaders of the future to do what Kent Amos does so well, or is his a particular talent that cannot be replicated or disseminated? Is his leadership effectiveness purely a force of his personality, or has he established criteria, methods, and practices that can be taught to others? What types of incentives and training can be offered to young leaders to encourage them to work with the children at greatest risk? Is it possible to develop similar programs for young people that do not require Amos's very high level of personal commitment, risk taking, and use of personal resources? And if so, are such programs likely to be as effective as his was in turning around the lives of such a large number of children?

CHAPTER THREE

ROBERT MOSES

The activist career of Robert Parris "Bob" Moses began during the era of traditional civil rights leadership and continues to the present day.[1] By 2000, at age sixty-five, Moses had spent his entire career working to improve the conditions of poor people in the nation's major cities and rural areas. What distinguishes him from his peers is his consistent effectiveness, based in part on his ability to switch gears and adapt his problem-solving methods to new realities and demands.

Moses came to national attention in 1961 when, as a leader in the grassroots Civil Rights movement, he fearlessly headed the voter registration campaign in Mississippi. He went south to volunteer in a nascent movement that reached its zenith in the 1964 Freedom Summer. Hundreds of college student volunteers went to Mississippi to work in Freedom Schools, where they tutored black children, organized the racially integrated Freedom Democratic Party that challenged the credentials of the racially segregated Democratic Party at the party convention in Atlantic City, and delivered free legal and health services to the poor. Freedom Summer's greatest contribution was that it opened up a closed society, exposing its racial discrimination to the rest of the nation. Mississippi would never be the same again. It was also a summer of major casualties: the murder of three volunteers—James Chaney, Mickey Schwerner, and Andrew Goodman—symbolized the repressive forces that the volunteers and staff were up against. However, the long-term results are that Mississippi now has the largest number of black elected officials of any state in the nation. In addition, after spending years away from the United States, Moses is back in his reluctant warrior role.

Moses is a quiet, self-effacing man; at one point in his life he changed his name to Robert Parris to publicly renounce the leadership mantle that had been placed on him. Now he seems to accept the public respect that has been accorded him for his substantial contributions. Moses left Mississippi in 1966 after five difficult years, which saw him shot at, beaten, and repeatedly arrested, and moved to Tanzania to teach math. (Before his civil rights activism, he was a doctoral student in mathematics at Harvard University and taught math at Horace Mann High School in New York City.) In Tanzania, Moses also coached boys' basketball.

Moses, his wife, Janet, and their four children moved back to Cambridge in the late 1970s so he could resume his graduate studies. They enrolled their children in the Cambridge public schools. In the African tradition, he and Janet developed a division of labor that involved him taking primary responsibility for their children's education while Janet assumed other duties. He became concerned that his oldest child, an eighth grader, was not studying algebra; the child's teacher explained that children at that age and grade level were not ready to study algebra. This contradicted Moses's experience: he had taught algebraic concepts to children who were even younger in Tanzania and recognized that in fact children are introduced to algebraic concepts in kindergarten and first grade.

Moses decided to tutor his daughter at home, but that did not solve the systemic problem—that all the other children in the King Open School were also denied the opportunity to learn mathematics at the age when they were ready to master the subject. Moses began to tutor other children, too, and soon he had organized a program not only to teach algebra but also to demystify math by having the children tackle complex mathematical problems using pictures and stories.[2] His pioneering work in finding effective methods to teach algebra to inner-city black boys especially had enormous success, success that challenged the prevailing myth—that young, black, inner-city males are the most difficult to teach. Over time, King graduates did so well in math that the superintendent of the Cambridge public schools decided that all sixth and seventh graders would be taught prealgebra and that all eighth graders would be taught algebra.[3]

Just as he had done in Mississippi with voting rights, Moses focused on ways to persuade his young charges, their parents, educators, foundation staff, and others that learning mathematics was not a mystical process. His gift for explaining the uncommon in common terms, and for developing strategies to teach these tools in an ordinary way, brought his pathbreaking work to national attention.[4] With foundation support, he organized curricula to teach the concepts in a national network of locally based projects.

Since its founding in 1982 (it was incorporated in 1991), the Algebra Project has served an estimated forty thousand students nationwide, including Boston, New York, Milwaukee, Indianapolis, Chicago, Oakland, Los Angeles, San Francisco, New Orleans, and Jackson, Mississippi. Its headquarters are located in Cambridge, Massachusetts. However, it is not accidental that Moses opened a second office in Jackson, Mississippi, where he is based. Eschewing administration, he has also returned to his first love, the classroom, teaching mathematics at Jim Hill High School.

Moses contends that citizenship now requires not only reading and writing skills but math and science as well and that it is critical that young people become mathematically literate if they expect to gain access to economic mobility. A systemic denial of these skills has brought about an educational crisis that subverts democratic equality and impairs citizenship in much the same way that the denial of voting rights did in the South a generation ago. Moses's premise is that algebra is a gateway subject, necessary for advancement to higher education. Urban school systems, however, are characterized by educational tracking, high dropout rates, poor teaching, and inadequate preparation in just this subject.

Using metaphorical language instead of memorization, the Algebra Project curriculum transforms the learning of essential mathematical skills into problem-solving methods. For example, bus lines and train routes are commonly used to explain the number line. Outbound and inbound bus routes help convey how numbers in algebra become positive or negative, depending on direction. Students are encouraged to solve problems, to formulate what they have learned in colloquial and then standard English, and finally to translate ordinary language into mathematical symbols. In the project's more recent African drums and ratios curriculum, students are taught how to construct their own instruments and to convert their knowledge of rhythmic meters into numerical intervals and proportions.[5]

At the center of the Algebra Project is the belief that young people must be empowered to advocate for their educational interests. Moses teaches his students to demand excellence from their teachers and to demand courses in the subjects they want to study. In this sense, he thinks of the Algebra Project as similar to the Civil Rights movement: just as civil rights advocates demanded the right to vote, students enrolled in the Algebra Project are taught to demand quality math education programs. Each focuses on the demand side. According to David Dennis, administrator of the Algebra Project, "One of the areas that we don't organize around very well is education. What we're trying to do with the Algebra Project is to let people know that you can increase the demand side."[6]

Dennis also notes that successful reform must involve the entire community, not only the students affected. This involves convincing parents and teachers to rid themselves of stereotypes—that certain children cannot compete. "The more horrific [fact] is that most of the teachers don't believe these kids can do this work."[7] Dennis cites a case in which the students in a high school in Jackson, Mississippi, advanced beyond the level their instructors were capable of teaching. The students then demanded that a teacher be hired from a nearby college to teach them at the level to which they had advanced. This contradicts the preconception that poor children do not want to learn, or cannot learn, at a rapid pace, or cannot reach a high level of achievement. It also presents a very different view of young people—as consumers who have found unique ways to use civic engagement to achieve on their own behalf. For Moses, educational opportunity is a frontline demand on today's civil rights agenda. Teaching high-order mathematical skills to these young people is a way to bridge the technological divide between those who have math skills and access to technology and those who do not. Moses contends that this is the issue that now separates the haves from the have-nots.

The work of Bob Moses, and David Dennis as well, demonstrates how effective leaders redefine the issues according to the needs of their constituents. These former sixties' activists are using the same strategies for organizing to empower individuals to demand educational excellence that they used to organize for voting rights. Moses sums up his strategy for achieving change in the lives of the young people he works with:

> The teacher is able to impress upon the child that learning is a function of effort, not of innate ability. The curriculum helps the students to raise their consciousness, so that they can affirm for themselves their own need for self-development. Such affirmations on their part are a critical prerequisite to confronting obstacles to their own development and acquiring attitudes and habits that will ensure success in many endeavors, including the Algebra Project.[8]

CHAPTER FOUR

EUGENE RIVERS

Eugene Rivers is one of the founders of Boston's Ten-Point Coalition, which was organized as a response to increased gang violence in the Roxbury and Dorchester communities.[1] The Ten-Point Coalition is an ecumenical group of street ministers that formed immediately after what came to be known as the Morning Star attack. The attack occurred in 1992 and involved the beating and repeated stabbing of twenty-one-year-old Jerome Brunson by fourteen hooded men outside the Morning Star Baptist Church. The men chased Brunson inside the church during the service for another young murder victim. Never before had violence reached such a level that it spilled over into a religious sanctuary.

At first the coalition ministers simply walked the streets at night with the gangs, talking to them, cajoling them, trying to develop their confidence and trust so they could help them turn their lives around, and become conforming citizens. It was not a traditional ministry for most of them, but it took Rivers back into familiar territory. He could speak the language of the gangs because he had once been a member of one in the rough streets of Philadelphia.

Called the "Savior of the Streets" by *Newsweek* magazine, Rivers is a charismatic leader with a gifted intellect and the oratorical style of a traditional Baptist preacher.[2] He can speak the language of the streets with the gang members as fluently as he advises the White House staff on policies to decrease urban crime.

Rivers's mother and his father separated when he was a toddler. His mother was a nurse; his father a member of the Nation of Islam who worked for its newspaper, *Muhammad Speaks*. Fortunately, at age sixteen, Rivers came under the influence of a Pentecostal minister who steered him away from the vicious cycle that entraps so many gang members. Subsequently, he studied for a while at Yale University and then at Harvard, though he never received a degree.[3] At Harvard, Rivers was instrumental in founding the Seymour Society, which is conservative in its religious beliefs but progressive in its social actions. By 1983, Rivers and Seymour Society members moved to live and work in some of Boston's poorest neighborhoods.[4]

Rivers also studied at the Eastern Baptist Theological Seminary.[5] His work is fundamentally grounded in his conservative religious beliefs, which he uses as an organizing tool. As much teacher as preacher, he speaks about the role that moral values can play in transforming the lives of the poor and the alienated.

Rivers's current base of operation is the Ella J. Baker House, a haven for crack addicts before it was restored to its Victorian elegance. It is painted in the red, green, and black colors that symbolize the black nationalism that its members also embrace. Located in a predominately African American and Latino neighborhood in the Dorchester section of Boston, it houses both the Azusa Christian Community, and several programs for at-risk youth.

Rivers applies religious teachings to solving social problems in a way reminiscent of Martin Luther King Jr. The message he offers young people is that they can and should turn their lives around not only because it is the Christian thing to do but also because it is the practical thing to do. If they do not leave the gangs, he tells them, their lives will always be at great risk. He works with them in the context of religiosity but is also mindful of the harsh environments they live in, realizing that before he can save their souls he has to keep them alive. He works with the police to save as many kids as possible.

He also challenges African American intellectuals to play a more active role in solving social problems:

Each day, 1,118 Black teenagers are victims of violent crime, 1,451 Black children are arrested, and 9,067 Black teenage girls get pregnant. A generation of Black males is drowning in its own blood in the prison camps that we euphemistically call "inner cities." Moreover, things are likely to get much worse. Some 40 years after the beginning of the Civil Rights movement, younger Black Americans are now growing up unqualified even for slavery. The result is a state of civil war, with children in violent revolt against the failed secular and religious leadership of the Black community. . . . What is the responsibility of Black intellectuals in the face of this nightmare?[6]

Not coincidentally, the work of the Azusa Christian Community and the secular work of the staff of the Ella J. Baker House overlap, because members of the Azusa Christian Community believe that, following the tradition of such activists as Dorothy Day, cofounder (with Peter Maurin) of the Catholic Worker Movement of the 1930s, a morally righteous Christian life requires that workers live with the poor who are their clients.[7]

Eva Thorne, a professor at Northeastern University, works with Rivers and the Azusa Christian Community. When the group moved into the Four Corners, a neighborhood in Dorchester, thirteen or fourteen years earlier, it was, she says, one of the most violent in Boston, with large numbers of territorially based gangs involved in the drug trade and violence. "We learned quickly that the only way we would be able to pursue our goal was to live and work among the poor and have our lives transformed as a result of our Christian commitment."[8]

However, the group soon discovered that it would not be effective in initiating change unless members learned to deal with the young, violent, male drug dealers in the neighborhood. "The only way to do that was to actually engage them," says Thorne. "Don't avoid them. Don't hide in the house. Don't expect the problem to just go away and dodge bullets as you run on about your business. Talk to them, and find out why they're doing this." A critical question for Azusa members was how the drug dealers succeeded in organizing and recruiting other young people.

Thorne, Rivers, and fellow Azusa members began their engagement with drug dealers by asking the chief dealer his advice on how to work with the other young people, those who looked to him as a role model. Thorne says,

This young man was brilliant. He had a computer system and subscriptions to Fortune 500 magazines. He was an avid reader. He had a few Swiss bank accounts. He had some contacts with the Cali [drug] cartel in Colombia. He knew that the way he was directing these kids into drug dealing and violence was not helpful. However, he didn't have people [in his life] who were willing to make sacrifices and put their lives on the line [for him].

The young man was willing to describe his method to Azusa members: "In the morning when Johnny goes to the corner for a loaf of bread, I'm there, and you're not. When you're at your job, and I'm standing out on the corner, I'm there, and you're not. When you come home and run from the subway station into your house to hide, I'm there, and you're not. I win, you lose." He and Azusa members had a series of conversations, some in crack houses. "We're here to work. We're not here to dictate, but we're here to learn. We're here to humble ourselves and to learn from you how we can be successful," they told him. They learned a great deal from him on how to conduct outreach with the kids, but they also learned that their effectiveness would rest on the extent to which they could gain the trust of the children.

Over time, the result of this initiative was a dramatic drop in gun violence related to drugs. Azusa made headway with both the head of the drug ring and his underlings: although some died and some went to prison, some did make it out of the gang. Thorne cautions, however, against glorifying this success: "What we're facing now is a new generation of younger, more violent drug dealers who are very, very different from the previous generation. . . . So as soon as people say we've won, we've succeeded—we're starting all over again. We are starting from scratch in Four Corners. We are starting from scratch with Azusa."

The Azusa Christian Community worked closely with a major police effort called Operation Ceasefire, launched by the Boston Police Department, the District Attorney's Office, the U.S. Attorney's Office, and the Massachusetts Department of Probation, among others. The purpose of Operation Ceasefire was to identify areas of gang activity, to inform gang members that they would be swiftly prosecuted for law violations, and to respond quickly to reported violations and other forms of trouble. Operation Ceasefire can be termed a success based on the numbers of youth homicides after its inception: between 1990 and 1994, there were 155 youth homicides in Boston; in 1995 and 1996, there were none.[9] Eugene Rivers readily acknowledges that the Ten-Point Coalition worked closely with Operation Ceasefire, negotiating, for example, with the police department to have youth offenders remanded to the Azusa Christian Community instead of being incarcerated.

The way members of the Ella J. Baker House immerse themselves in the local community is consistent with both the philosophy and the organizing tools of the late Ella J. Baker, for whom the house is named. Baker was known for involving local people in the decisionmaking process and for trying to understand them within the context of their environment. Baker, an African American woman with a lengthy career as a human rights activist, was field secretary to the National Association for the Advancement of Colored People in the 1940s, an organizer for the Montgomery bus boycott in 1955, the first executive director of the Southern Christian Leadership Conference, and a catalyst for organizing the Student Nonviolent Coordinating Committee in 1960.[10] Summer programs at the Ella J. Baker House range from a "boot camp" (modeled after Outward Bound) for very troubled youth, a summer Freedom School, and a music camp.

Rivers's philosophy is shared by many African American individuals, churches and other faith-based organizations, and civic, fraternal, and voluntary associations, who agree that the values and the institutions that once were the bastion of stability for black families and neighborhoods have eroded. They thus emphasize values education as a vehicle for solving social problems affecting black communities. The practice of blaming government for not fixing all the problems is being met with less and less acceptance. Taking responsibility for one's actions, for the behavior of one's offspring, and ultimately for one's community is gaining ground. The culture of victimization is viewed as inappropriate—and counterproductive—to the aims of today's reformers.

Rivers does not abide fools gladly, nor does he countenance deviant and criminal behavior. He is especially harsh on black-on-black crime. His years of experience on the streets of Boston have shown him how cruel young people can be to each other and how many violent acts are committed over inconsequential things: a leather jacket, a pair of brand-name sneakers. He is unrelenting in his call for constructive engagement by blacks— not only local residents but also the black middle class—to tackle the problems of inner-city communities. He believes it is the responsibility of all black people to rebuild black civil societies, which have been torn apart by the consequences of poverty and violence. In his view, the first modern major constructive effort was the Civil Rights movement, in which, however, the fight for freedom and justice was relatively straightforward. Rivers notes:

> Freedom was principally a matter of rights. . . . But a new vision cannot simply address relations of Black citizens to the broader political community and the state. As American politics devolves and inner-city life degenerates, our vision must also be about the relations within our communities: about Black families and the importance of parental responsibilities to the health of those families, the evil of Black-on-Black violence, the stupidity of defining Black culture around anti-Semitism or other forms of racial and ethnic hatred, the value of education and intellectual achievement, the importance of mutual commitment and cooperative effort, and the essential role of personality morality and of religious conviction in defining that morality.[11]

According to Rivers, Boston spends $24 million a year on violence prevention that, he believes, promotes negative images of young black men. Consistent with Rivers's belief in the community being involved in such policy issues, he thinks that local residents should also be involved in the legislative process, insisting, for example, that funds be redirected from bullets, nightsticks, and stun guns into after-school programs and science, math, and cultural-education programs "to which kids are sentenced as a condition of parole."[12] Rivers is gearing up for Operation 2006, which is the year that census projections predict a 27 percent increase in the at-risk youth population. By then, Rivers expects to have a thousand churches working with high-risk young people in the most troubled neighborhoods.

Rivers explains the nexus among poverty, racism, and violence. "Poor, inner-city Black folks suffer largely from 'spiritual ignorance, lack of discipline and disorganization' [that] is exacerbated by, but is no longer caused by, racism/White supremacy." Children with guns are "angry about the disappointment in their lives. A generation or more of absent fathers, angry mothers, and shortsighted leaders have ailed today's young people." He calls it "a Franz Fanon nightmare—the violence of the oppressed being played out on themselves."[13]

For Rivers the core around which solutions can be created and applied is religious faith, the same religious faith that has sustained generations of African Americans through great difficulty. "It's the only thing that goes deep with black people. Besides, it's all that's left. Social programs and the Civil Rights movement are history. Poor people are morally obligated to fight for themselves. That fight includes turning to the redemptive power of Jesus Christ to rekindle faith, hope, and a moral center."[14]

CHAPTER FIVE

DEFINING MOMENTS AND OTHER INFLUENCES

A career as an agent of social change, in the tradition of these transformative leaders, requires a special type of individual: one willing to take extraordinary risks by pursuing change in the midst of often formidable opposition. Many people who go into these careers have a clear sense of mission, an approach that offsets the disappointments, disadvantages, and other difficulties they encounter. The stories of other new urban leaders follow.

Jeffrey Brown

Jeffrey Brown, a Harvard-trained Baptist minister, a graduate of Andover Newton Theological Seminary, and a doctoral student in American church history, had been pastor of Union Baptist Church in Cambridge, Massachusetts, for eight or nine years when he was confronted with a crisis that transformed his life.[1] In January 1990, Jessie McKie, twenty-one, and Rigoberto Carrion, thirty, were stabbed to death about fifty yards from Brown's church when McKie refused to give his leather jacket to "Four Corners" gang members. McKie ran to the church after he was stabbed but found it locked. Had the doors been open, Brown believes, these young lives might have been spared. "I took it as a sign that I had to change my mission," he says.

Brown's dream as a seminary student had been to build and lead a "whopping big church"—known in the faith community as a megachurch. This dream changed quickly after the murders, giving way to a spiritual calling that took Brown into the dangerous streets of Boston to minister to gang members. He moved away from the safe haven of Union Baptist Church as well as from the renown that would have followed from achieving his original career goal. Brown recalled, "I guess for me that was an indication that if I am going to be engaged in the kind of ministry to build a community, it would never be to build a large, middle-class congregation. It would be part of the force for social change in my own community."

Brown joined an interdenominational group of clergy that, after another murder near a church, established the Ten-Point Coalition.[2] "There had always been this unspoken rule that what was going on out in the streets, you didn't bring that stuff into the sanctuary," says Brown. "The Morning Star incident illustrated the willingness of some young people to cross that line, to basically 'dis' [disrespect] the church." Thus the decision to take the church into the streets. What began as an isolated incident, the killing of Jessie McKie, had long-lasting consequences for Brown. It propelled him to center stage as a leader concerned about the destruction of children in inner cities. The Ten-Point Coalition's work has been cited prominently in the media, and the program has been replicated in other cities affected by gang violence.

Brown has cast his lot with poor, troubled young people. Jeffrey Brown represents a new generation of urban clergy who have adopted a social gospel as their calling, taking it into the streets, where so many troubled youth can be found, rather than waiting for them to come into the churches. He is also part of a larger faith-based movement—including the Interfaith Network— that works with urban youth.

James Capraro

James Capraro, one of the few whites in this study, is a native Chicagoan whose organization, the Greater Southwest Development Corporation, promotes economic development on Chicago's West Side.[3] The impetus for Capraro's social change work came early in his life:

> There's a chapter in a book by Studs Turkel titled "The Park" which was an interview Turkel wrote based on a day in my life when I was sixteen years old.[4] That afternoon, Martin Luther King Jr. was marching through Market Park [in Chicago] and met with a horrific response from white extremists. I grew up a block and a half from Market Park and ended up in the park that day. I was not very politically aware. I had been walking around when I saw a bunch of police officers in the neighborhood, and they were all going to the park because something was happening there. I chased the police officers as a kid might chase a fire truck or an ambulance, just to see what was going on. I was kind of sorry I saw what was going on—but not really. I think I was happy I saw what was going on. That day was just so unsettling and downright ugly that it made me, as a sixteen-year-old

person, become interested in something more than the White Sox and girls, which was about the total of my interest at the time. I decided that somebody had to think about neighborhood change and neighborhood deterioration and be on the side of right as opposed to the side of wrong. I saw a lot of people on the side of wrong that day.

What Capraro witnessed was Martin Luther King's early incursion into northern civil rights activity. Before King's campaigns in Chicago and Cicero, Illinois, the major protest demonstrations had been in the Deep South.

King led a demonstration through the neighborhood for open housing—this was an all-white neighborhood at the time. It was a white working-class neighborhood where lots of folks worked in factories or drove buses or worked for the postal service. They were predominantly blue-collar. He was met with violent resistance. I remember him walking down Sixty-Seventh Street with a number of protestors, and people were throwing bricks and bottles. I remember people identifying the cars of the people who were with him and setting them on fire. I remember an African American couple was surrounded by a jeering mob because they were driving through the neighborhood and got stopped at a stoplight at Sixty-Seventh and California Avenue. They were rocking the car, and a young girl jumped up on the hood and started kicking at the windshield. The people inside were totally terrorized.

That's what happened that day. At first, I couldn't sleep. I thought, gee, everything the nuns taught me in grade school is wrong. This isn't the greatest country in the world, and not everybody can grow up to be president. It just kind of shook the very foundation of what I thought being American was about. I kind of carried that with me. I was unsettled, I was confused, and I was sixteen and a junior in high school—actually the summer between my sophomore and junior years. Two years later I graduated and I ended up in night school, working in a factory during the day and going to college at night—and became an antiwar organizer.

Capraro's career as an organizer was defined by experiences that challenged his belief system. Capraro was attempting to reconcile the dissonance between Roman Catholic teachings on racial equality and the violence of the demonstrators. The essential issue Capraro wrestled with was the question of who would stand up on the side of right.

Freeman Hrabowski III

Freeman Hrabowski III, a mathematician and president of the University of Maryland, Baltimore County, is a product of the Birmingham, Alabama, public schools and the son of an educator. Born in 1950 in Birmingham, Hrabowski graduated at age nineteen from Hampton Institute (now Hampton University) with highest honors in mathematics; at twenty-four he received his doctorate. As a child in 1963, Hrabowski was fire-hosed and arrested during the Martin Luther King–led Birmingham civil rights demonstrations.[5] He also had the distinction of being the youngest student arrested in those protest demonstrations.

Hrabowski, instead of following a career path as a research scientist, became a higher education administrator and has used his position as a university president to bridge the racial divide by increasing the number of minorities in scientific professions. He is author of the book, *Beating the Odds: Raising Academically Successful African American Males.*[6]

Hrabowski explains why he started his program:

A large number of black students were not doing well. Because of black student protests, I tried to figure out what was bothering the students. While there was, of course, some racism and elitism, what I found when I did an

*Freeman
Hrabowski III*

assessment of academic performance was that the average black male GPA [grade point average] was 1.9 and black female [average] was barely 2.0. Almost half the African American students on this campus were on probation. Yet when I talked to them, nobody talked about how they were doing in school. I'd ask, "How are you doing," and they'd say, "Fine." I also found that a large number of white students were also not doing well. We needed to look at the culture of the campus and particularly at [how we worked] with freshmen, which professors taught those students, and the way we thought about the freshman-year experience. So we began with [the question], What did we need to do to improve the performance of African Americans?

Hrabowski's childhood exposure to racial injustice combined with his academic training in the sciences came together to influence him to decrease the high failure rates of black students and to increase the numbers of high-achieving black males. His "calling" is subtler than that of Jeffrey Brown or of Kent Amos, but it is just as viable.

Allan and Susan Tibbles

Allan and Susan Tibbles, founders and codirectors of the New Song Urban Ministries in Baltimore, exemplify leaders whose service springs from their religious beliefs.[7] They are a married white couple who, in 1991, made a conscious choice to live and work among poor African Americans in a Baltimore neighborhood called Sandtown. Their decision to live in a poor inner-city neighborhood was based on their deep commitment to Christianity.

Ours was a faith-based motivation when we came here, because we believed that as Christian believers in the Bible we were called to use the gifts and the resources that we have been blessed with to be among people who had not been given the same kinds of resources. It was basically acting on a principle of Christian community development that was articulated first by a man named John Perkins, an African American who was involved in the Civil Rights movement.

According to the Tibbleses, Perkins's ideas center on three guiding principles: relocation, redistribution, and reconciliation. First, successful people should relocate to communities whose residents lack such basics as food, shelter, and clothing. Second, there should be a redistribution of resources, so that those who do not have life's necessities would be able to share the resources of those with an excess of them. Third, racial conflicts between whites and blacks should be reconciled. The Tibbleses believe that reconciliation should be sought intentionally and with foresight. This does not mean moving blacks into white communities, since this simply causes reverse migration. Rather, reconciliation should involve whites moving into black neighborhoods and becoming neighbors and partners so that the two groups can build together.

The Tibbleses gained the trust of their new neighbors by interacting with neighborhood children, thus establishing the couple as stable members of the community. The couple then organized a small church in their home, which allowed them to develop good relationships with the children's parents and guardians. Then they worked to establish a school, a health center, and a chapter of Habitat for Humanity, the latter enabling them to form a home ownership program. Out of these efforts evolved a comprehensive community development project aimed at transforming impoverished Sandtown. The Tibbleses' organization fosters strong linkages among Sandtown residents, who teach at the school, attend the church, and participate in other community activities.

One of the challenges for people like Susan and Allan Tibbles is that their new neighbors often expect them to solve all of their problems. The Tibbleses are aware that this path not only would lead to burnout for them but, worse, would undermine their neighbors' independence and empowerment. Their aim is to encourage Sandtown residents to see themselves not as victims but as partners in the neighborhood's revitalization project. Another challenge is to stay focused on a clearly defined mission, no matter how urgent the day-to-day problems.

The couple's approach, whichwas to create an interracial collaboration for rebuilding a low-income community, is well suited for replication. Working in a small community allows organizers to establish close bonds with residents, to empower residents to work for the community's welfare, and to foster a partnership so that residents can continue to work on the issues when the organizers leave. Organizing community residents to promote the good of the community and including them in the decisionmaking process both engenders a sense of unity among the residents and empowers them to act in their own—and their communities'—behalf.

Thomas Stewart

As director of SEED charter school, an inner-city boarding school in Washington, D.C., Thomas Stewart is deeply involved with providing quality education to some of the city's poorest children.[8] He was once one of them, he says, and his involvement "stems from a couple of critical personal experiences, and two professional revelations."

> Part of my upbringing involved spending some time in foster care in the District of Columbia's Junior Village. I was there for a couple of years, and I was left with a question for most of my life, especially during my childhood and adolescent years: What's wrong with my family? What's wrong with me? Why did we end up in this place? Dysfunctional families seem to be disproportionately involved with [the foster care system]. I think my life's purpose is to help families.

That Stewart turned his painful personal experiences into his life's cause and occupation is fortunate for the children who benefit from his mission. Stewart graduated from the University of the District of Columbia, received a scholarship to do his doctoral studies in political science at Harvard, and worked with the Boston Camp and Mobilization Project and also a project designed to involve parents in public education (as little as 10 percent of parents were involved in their children's schools, he found).

Stewart recalls his training at Harvard:

> We talked a lot about institutions in the courses, political institutions, public and private. No one ever talked much about prisons, which were salient institutions in my community. I always thought that I would go to prison. [The assertions that describe] prison as a deterrent, for example, just weren't true. In my neighborhood, people wanted to go. It was a badge of honor to have prison on your per-

sonal résumé. I always felt deprived that I never had that experience. So I took advantage of the dissertation research opportunity, received good funding, and interviewed over a hundred inmates. My dissertation had two components. I first wanted to look at the history of prisons in America and focus on their impact on urban areas. Then I did a case study in which I looked at two neighborhoods in Boston: South Boston, which is predominantly Irish, and Roxbury, which is a portion of Dorchester, a predominantly black area of the city. I was amazed to hear these guys tell stories that were so similar to my own, in terms of their family situations and their experiences at school.

After completing his doctorate, Stewart returned to Washington and is now using his training, skills, and insight to work with economically disadvantaged children, who have the opportunity to live in a nurturing, safe, family-style environment while enrolled in a competitive college preparatory high school.

SEED Charter School, located near Union Station, is one of the nation's first public college prep and boarding schools that offers a rigorous curriculum and a host of after-school enrichment programs. The education offered is a counterweight to some of the disadvantages the children bring with them: poverty, unstable homes, and communities. The students live on campus nine months of the year; they go home one weekend a month in addition to holiday breaks and the three months when school is not in session. SEED students focus on what Stewart refers to as the basics: math, science, geography, literature, and social studies. In addition to this core curriculum, students are taught good study skills and advanced computer skills. And because this is a residential school and functions as the students' home, a broad array of after-school activities is offered.

Hattie Dorsey

Some individuals are drawn to social change occupations because of the commitment they have observed in their parents and in other role models. An example of this type of modeling is Hattie Dorsey, director of the Atlanta Neighborhood Development Partnership (ANDP).[9] She chose a career that involves helping underserved populations because of the activism of her father:

> He was a Baptist minister who worked at the Tabernacle Baptist Church during the Civil Rights movement. I am a preacher's daughter. I watched his activism, and it began to make sense when I left home and moved to Washington, to work on Capitol Hill for a congressman. I was the first black person hired on Capitol Hill by a Georgia congressman. They went through this process of looking for a qualified black person, and there was pressure being applied from Atlanta [to hire a black person in the U.S. Congress]. The standard response was they could not find anyone who was qualified. My father, who was an activist and who was known to all the politicians, said, "I have a daughter working in Washington, D.C., and I don't think you can come back to me with the statement that she is not qualified."
>
> I was called in for an interview, and I got the job. A large part of it was because they could not figure out how

to go back and tell my father I was not qualified. I think in that experience I learned why my father was pushing for [civil rights] and how the laws of the land affected what happened down there in the base of the community.

Hattie
Dorsey

Following her work as a congressional aide, Dorsey held several highly influential positions in the public and private sectors. One job required Dorsey to establish a model job-training program for minority youth in California. Dorsey's program, underwritten by corporate funds, has since been replicated by the state. The ANDP, Dorsey's current employer, is one of the nation's fastest growing local intermediaries between community development corporations and lenders. With financial help from the private sector and the philanthropic community, the ANDP provides financial and technical assistance to more than a dozen community development corporations in Atlanta and Cobb County, Georgia. The partnership has played a major role in the creation of more than 5,000 new or renovated affordable housing units. The Imperial Hotel, which is undergoing a $9.2 million conversion into apartments for the homeless and working poor, is a beneficiary of ANDP's work.

The ANDP was included in the Human Capital Development Initiative, a plan by the National Congress for Community Economic Development to recruit a thousand new staff members and volunteers to help rebuild low-income communities. The initiative has ten pilot programs in thirteen communities nationwide.

The ANDP works on housing and community development through the Community Redevelopment Loan and Investment Fund, which finances community revitalization projects. A subset of the ANDP is the Community Development Institute. The Human Capital Development Institute is a partner with Clark–Atlanta University, which focuses on instruction and workshops for community leaders, lenders, and representatives from the corporate sector involved in community revitalization projects.

Conclusion

The phenomenon of a chance encounter shaping one's life mission and work is characteristic of leaders across the boundaries of training, geography, and race. Life-altering events strike responsive chords in individual hearts. These events inform a person's perspective on what the communal needs are, on the way to live one's life, and whether one could derive meaning from work that did not heed a calling. It is unlikely that Jeffrey Brown would have made a dramatic change in his life, especially in his career goal, had he not learned firsthand the extent to which the children with whom he worked needed him. Similarly, James Capraro's adolescent chance encounter with racial hostility set him on a path to erase as much conflict as possible by working to improve the living conditions of Chicago's poor.

Hattie Dorsey's social change career is an outgrowth of the values imparted primarily by her father. Others, like the Tibbleses, were influenced by their faith-based beliefs, which they wove into their community development work. Such leaders come to pursue their life's mission not because of an intense personal awakening but because they truly believe that the only way to live a fulfilling and value-centered life is by giving and helping those in dire need.

PART TWO

STRATEGIES
AND VISION

CHAPTER SIX

THE INTERNAL CHANGE STRATEGY

The approach of the new urban leaders to the problems of the black urban underclass differs from that of the older generation of black leaders, whose work concentrated on stemming the effects of white racial prejudice. Many in the younger generation, on the other hand, believe that these problems are manifestations of a crisis among blacks. Individual behavior such as the sale of and addiction to drugs; black-on-black crime; and high rates of incarceration are viewed as symptoms of this crisis. Other quality-of-life problems these leaders address are how to provide education and marketable skills, strengthen fragile families living in poverty, and prevent black middle-class families from moving to the suburbs.

Major national crises such as the one now afflicting the black underclass once justified social welfare policies. The Great Depression of the 1930s led to the nation's first massive social welfare programs, under Franklin

Delano Roosevelt's New Deal. The Social Security Act of 1935, for example, was meant to insure Americans against the loss of wages due to death, widowhood, retirement, and disability. The second major federal social welfare legislation, in the 1960s, was enacted under Lyndon Johnson's Great Society— for example, the act establishing the Office of Economic Opportunity and other programs designed to reduce poverty and racial discrimination through early childhood intervention, job training, housing, cash transfers, and the like. No third generation of social welfare policy on the magnitude of the New Deal and the Great Society has occurred.[1]

Without massive federal support for human welfare programs, the new urban leaders have had to find other resources and invent other strategies to respond to the human welfare needs of their constituencies. Although there is perhaps no agreement on exact strategy, practice, or vision, there is among these leaders a strong bias toward finding solutions based on empowerment of individuals and communities to practice self-reliance, a method that might be termed the "internal change" strategy. Such a strategy works on the individual level, the premise being that problems often stem from the poor choices that individuals make and that these individuals need to link these choices with the outcomes. Therefore, reform focuses on decreasing an individual's harmful behavior, the behavior that minimizes that individual's chances for success. For example, responsible personal behavior means that one does not place oneself at risk of too-early parenthood by participating in premarital sexual activities. The programs of some nonprofit organizations thus center on changing individuals' choices through changing their values and through emphasizing that destructive values—and the choices they lead to—result in negative outcomes. These programs operate without outside funding. They depend on moral suasion rather than foundation or government grants. Examples include the "Rite of Passage" programs for adolescents sponsored by black churches and civic organizations.

An underlying assumption of the internal change strategy is that a culture of victimization has replaced the culture, once deeply rooted in black families, of self-reliance. Critics of the culture of victimization propose that children be socialized to accept personal responsibility and that adults who rely too heavily on the largess of others, be it government programs or private philanthropy, be encouraged to bear personal responsibility. Groups such as Concerned Black Men, which has chapters in several cities, teach young black males how to practice responsible reproductive behavior. The Alliance of Black Men, in Washington, D.C., effectively disarmed gang members responsible for murders in a public housing project and subsequently organized job training and found employment for former gang members. In numerous programs, older black men and women mentor their younger peers on how to be responsible and productive spouses, parents, workers, and citizens.

The internal change strategy is rooted in the heritage of the black church; the leading proponents of the strategy are faith-based organizations. The most enduring values of black families have traditionally been an unwavering belief in God and the concept of redemption. The problems of alcoholism and substance abuse, teen pregnancy and violence, were considered "sins" against the religious teachings. "Sinners" were required to ask God and the church's congregation for forgiveness before they could be embraced again by the community of believers. This religious belief system served to bind communities together, to maintain social control over those who deviated from the accepted standards, and to force those individuals to publicly acknowledge wrongdoing. In the most orthodox churches, members were expected to faithfully follow the Ten Commandments. The church, therefore, was the source of the ethics and values that guided conduct outside the religious sphere.

Various programs have sprung up to reinstate these long-held values. The Links, a black women's service organization, sponsors High Expectations, which teaches values and high self-esteem to teenage girls. Best Friends, for example, aggressively promotes sexual abstinence as a value to be embraced by the teenage girls in the program.[2] The Children's Defense Fund, led by Marian Wright Edelman, emphasizes the role of religious and spiritual values in molding healthy young people and operates an annual religious institute at its facility at the Alex Haley Farm near Knoxville, Tennessee. It has also developed curriculum materials for teaching values.

Traditionally, the field of American social welfare has not given a significant role to spirituality in rehabilitating individuals and in solving social problems, and social welfare practitioners usually do not incorporate spirituality into their work. This, however, is changing as some who work on the front lines of poor urban communities factor in the erosion of spirituality and the decline of religion as underlying causes of some urban problems. Robert Woodson, whose work on affordable housing, gang violence, and black entrepreneurship earned him the MacArthur "genius" award in 1998, is a strong advocate of infusing religion into the quest for solutions to urban problems. Charles Colson, staff member in the Nixon White House, is another advocate of this position. His program, Prison Ministries, has been successful in reducing the recidivism rate of inmates through the practice of faith-based rehabilitation.[3]

Increasingly, many urban drug treatment programs are incorporating a spiritual dimension into their work with substance abusers.

When asked to identify the most critical problems facing these communities, Woodson does not cite poverty or unemployment or poor housing, health care, or education. "The most pressing problems facing urban low-income people," he says, "are moral and spiritual. . . . The gang kids and prostitutes that we have turned around are examples of God's grace in action. They are moral people, who say, 'I used to be a hooker, I used to do this stuff [drugs]. But God has entered my life. Now, let me demonstrate it another way.'"[4]

Robert
Woodson

Woodson has not always used the faith-based rehabilitation approach. Earlier in his career he was a civil rights activist in Philadelphia and Chester, Pennsylvania. He received a master's degree in social work from the University of Pennsylvania and worked for the National Urban League. Perhaps a reason for his shift in approach came from having little success when trying to rehabilitate individuals through conventional methods. Woodson began to contemplate what the fundamental issues really were. The traditional therapeutic interventions for drug addicts that have not been effective with crack cocaine addicts, and the increase in youth violence, for example, have left reformers with fewer tools. Moreover, lack of in-house drug treatment has caused reformers to look elsewhere for solutions. Reformers are questioning the methodologies and theories and underlying causes they were taught—and that have worked in the past. There also are few traditional explanations for why young people who have had material advantages still turn to drugs and other social harms. These, too, may be caused by a spiritual void. Woodson explains:

The presence of drugs and guns would not create a killer and drug addict in your home. . . . So the answer is not to concentrate on getting the drugs and the guns out of the communities. The answer is to give the people a deeper meaning. What distinguishes the poor people in places like Bishop McCullough's [House of Prayer for All People] housing development [in Washington, D.C.] or the Muslim community in Philadelphia on Fifty-Second and Parkside is that they have morals, they have values, they have beliefs. You have a whole community of people who are clean and decent. They don't have a better education. So if morals, values, and beliefs are where the problems exist, then why don't we concentrate on addressing the problems where they exist?

The focus on values and morality puts the emphasis on the transformation rather than the rehabilitation of dysfunctional individuals and communities. The rehabilitation approach emerges from the medical model—first identifying the pathology and then prescribing the cure. The values-centered—or transformation—approach, on the other hand, rejects the medical model, adopting instead religious principles and values. Practitioners speak of the change that occurs in the hearts of their constituents. They speak of the religious values that give individuals a framework for behavior and that prevent them from returning to addiction or crime or other deviant or problematic behavior. To return to such a life-style would violate their religious commitments to a higher power or to God. According to Woodson, "Such . . . programs do not simply curb deviant behavior but also offer something more—a fulfilling life that eclipses the power of temptation. Upon entering their old environment, such transformed individuals have not only been able to resist its temptations but have actually been able to affect the surroundings."

Value-laden approaches to solving urban problems are becoming increasingly popular for a number of reasons. First, more faith-based organizations are working in urban communities trying to solve complex problems. The clergy is taking a far more aggressive role in promoting an activist theology that emphasizes a secular approach to religion. This work follows the tradition of Martin Luther King Jr. and other clergymen, especially the community activist clergy, who advocate that biblical injunctions be applied to the secular world. Second, government programs for the poor have been phased out or underfunded, placing pressure on nonprofit organizations, including the faith-based, to become involved in solving problems facing local communities. Third, even social problems perceived as behavioral or structural (drug abuse, unemployment, lack of affordable housing and good schools) respond to a focus on changes in personal behavior. As Robert Woodson says,

> We have spent trillions of dollars trying to change the structure of the society for the poor. Altering the physical conditions of the environment will not have a transformational effect on the person's behavior. You take a pig, put it in a Hilton, he'll create a pigpen. You take an entrepreneur, you put him a pigpen, and he'll create a pig farm. The difference here is the values and beliefs of the person. A transformed heart needs busy hands and a full stomach. Therefore, once that person has been transformed, it is easier to sustain him. Each individual needs a job, a decent place to live, and a safe environment. We haven't gotten that right. We placed all our emphasis on the one and on none of the others. What is needed is balance. . . . You must first transform the person before you reward that person. I use as an example the prodigal son. You know when he was selfish and said, "Give me my fortune," and went into the world, the father remained calm—like a lighthouse. And the boy went into the world and squandered all his wealth. And then it was said that he was feeding pigs.

Then Woodson adds,

> An interesting line in the Bible says, "And no one would give him anything." And the next line is, "And then he

came to himself." When he came to himself, he was contrite. And when he came back to his father, he said, "I am not worthy to be thy son." However, suppose the father does what most poverty programs do, which is to rush to him at the bar where he's drinking and hanging out, and say, "Here's a job for you. Here's the ring."

Woodson's view—that individuals should practice personal responsibility, humility, and high moral and religious values—has its roots in the traditional values of the African American culture. It has a significant following among other urban leaders. According to Eva Thorne, a member of the Azusa Christian Community, protégé of Eugene Rivers, and a professor at Northeastern University, lack of deeply entrenched values is what sets the gang members with whom she works apart from the mainstream inner-city culture. Some of these young people, Thorne has discovered, are born into their fathers' gangs. She describes these particular children as more violent and more willing to engage in law-breaking behavior than gang members the Azusa Community has worked with earlier. Her conclusion is that

> what is needed are outreach programs, more civic engagement, and the teachings as basic as Jesus loves little children and to treat people right. That inculcation of values and morals is very critical. The root of the problem is a lack of hope. They have a lack of vision for the future—and for the rest of their lives. [They are experiencing] the loss of faith and hope, the death of faith and hope. The Old Testament says that where there is no vision, the people perish. I see a lot of that among the kids here, who have no vision for their lives, no sense of what their promise or potential might be.[5]

The inability of these young people to envision their potential prevents them from shunning gang involvement, staying in school, envisioning going to college and having legitimate careers. Azusa Christian Community members live and work among these young people and have taken them on as their mission. Their religious faith sustains them as they continue to look for ways to transform this second generation of young gang members.

Highly experienced leaders like Eugene Rivers and Robert Woodson have worked in the field long enough to understand that effective strategies do not necessarily remain effective indefinitely. New problems, such as second-generation gang members, present new challenges and require new solutions. The call for moral and spiritual teachings to transform the individual is a higher order perspective, which these leaders believe eclipses traditional approaches.

Woodson is representative of what appears to be a growing group of critics of government-sponsored social programs who argue that the traditional strategy of using huge amounts of government funding for programs to ameliorate urban problems is the wrong approach. Faith-based activists employ, instead, a combination of morality-based and skills-building approaches. They believe that they must teach character and also marketable skills to help these young people succeed in life—that is, if they can gain their trust and hold their attention long enough to do so.

The Decline of the Black Family

The new urban leaders believe that many urban problems can be traced to the decline of the black family and the erosion of its time-honored values, traditions, and economic stability.

Families that cannot provide adequately for their children do not have the means to counter the hostile forces that undermine self-sufficiency. The geographical and economic mobility of the black middle class and the subsequent decline of formerly tight-knit neighborhoods have undermined the viability of the fragile families left behind. Never-married single parents are among the most vulnerable urban poor, and they account for the fastest growing newly established households. A disproportionate number live in poverty.

Lloyd Smith, founder of the Marshall Heights Community Development Corporation and currently chairman of the National Capital Revitalization Corporation in Washington, D.C., asserts that "personal responsibility is not the government's problem. The government doesn't conceive the children."[6] Smith reflects on how he and his wife reared their children. "I have four daughters, and none ever brought me a child out of wedlock, because they know this is not what you do in our family. They've never been on drugs, and I've never had to go to jail [to intervene] for any of my five children, including my son. They're all members of the church and they've got [good] values."

When asked to explain what distinguishes his grown children from those not faring as well today, he says, "I didn't make a lot of excuses [for their behavior]. They came home complaining about the nuns at their parochial school," and he told them, "They're not beating you. They're not mistreating you." In effect, he was in accord with the type of education and discipline used by those to whom he entrusted the education of his children.

Thaddeus Lott, superintendent of the Houston Unified Charter School District, identifies the erosion of two critical institutions that have had an adverse impact on the welfare of the children he serves: the family and the community.[7] He and Smith cite such parental support of teachers as an example of what used to occur when black middle-class families still lived in the inner cities. Those left behind are the very poor, who have far less involvement in the schools and ability to strengthen them. Lott observes that some of these parents give their children material things, such as brand-name clothing and sneakers, to fill the void left by a lack of community and school involvement. This is their way to give their children better lives than they had. Lott says, "But the children don't know why they're getting [these things]. They're not the ones denied; we were. And if you're going to buy some Air Jordans, you ought to be buying them for yourself. You were the ones who did without the shoes when you were growing up, not your kids."

A similar point is made by Freeman Hrabowski III, founder of the University of Maryland's Meyerhoff Program, which seeks to increase the number of black males in the sciences. Hrabowski finds that the most effective parents are proactive, who push their children to do their best in their academic work, parents who work to balance the negative influences from television, the streets, and the schools. Hrabowski notes that many young parents who gave birth to their children when they were teenagers "have not been taught the importance of being strict and demanding . . . while loving their children at the same time. We've become much too lax in our approach."[8] Some of these less-prepared parents set their children up for failure by their unrealistic idea of success, teaching their children to aspire to careers as professional athletes and entertainers instead of the traditional occupations obtainable with a college degree.

Structural Problems in the Inner City

A criticism of individual transformation is that there is no built-in capacity to change public policies and to rectify structural problems and that, therefore, government and privately sponsored ventures in economic development will always be needed. Pablo Eisenberg, founder of the Center for Community Change in Washington, D.C., is particularly concerned about the long-term effects of joblessness and redlining over past decades.[9] When financial institutions used discriminatory practices to systematically deny mortgages, loans, and other financial services to the inner city (redlining), it placed another obstacle in the path to upward mobility for the black underclass. Inner-city residents had difficulty buying their own homes or starting their own businesses in their neighborhoods. The barrier to investment kept these people from achieving economic stability and their neighborhoods from becoming economically viable. When home ownership was an achievable goal of inner-city residents, their neighborhoods flourished, leading to the development of stable inner-city institutions. Residential redlining prevented this development. It also caused potential homeowners to remain renters, often at exorbitant rates for substandard housing. Commercial redlining kept many services and supplies from being available locally—or only at very high prices—and required residents to travel some distance to shop.

Redlining became illegal with the passage of the Community Reinvestment Act (CRA), a federal law passed in 1977 prohibiting banks from refusing to lend in low- and moderate-income communities. The law puts the onus on the banks to either grant loans in these neighborhoods or defend their refusal, stating that "regulated financial institutions have a continuing and affirmative obligation to help meet the credit needs of the local communities in which they are chartered."[10]

Eisenberg also points to the necessity of job creation for black inner-city residents on the assumption "that the private sector can never create sufficient jobs." He advocates "a supplementary, major, public service employment program." These programs might be similar to two Depression-era programs—the Works Progress Administration (WPA) and the Civilian Conservation Corps (CCC)—and the more recent Comprehensive Employment and Training Act (CETA). The WPA provided government jobs for millions of the unemployed during the 1930s. The CCC had a twofold mission: to reduce unemployment, especially among young men, and to preserve the nation's natural resources.[11] CETA was a 1973 government program that provided block grants to state and local governments for public and private job training and for such youth programs as the Job Corps and Summer Youth Employment.

A Marshall Plan for the Inner City

The urban leaders interviewed are careful to point out that some low-income black families are doing relatively well. Those at the very bottom of the socioeconomic scale—the black underclass—are doing quite poorly, however. According to Dick Boone, with the Tides Foundation Program on Participatory Democracy in Santa Barbara, California,

> There probably has not been enough attention [given] to the upward mobility of blacks and the creation of a new black middle class. The result is what I call the "residue

problem." The population that has not yet escaped the poor communities [poses the problem], and has many important factors associated with it. The first factor is race. More than any other single factor, race has been a generic problem. The color of the skin produces fear. Another reason is the history of the black family in this country. . . . [and] . . . the disappearance of the black male. All of these things reinforce what I call the residue population, the population that hasn't escaped. Then add to that, more recently, the crime problem that is largely associated with drugs and induces fear on the part of others, of black males. This causes a further isolation and continuation of the walls being built around that part of the population.[12]

Boone notes that the greatest failures to solve the crisis in the black urban communities are (1) the problem of sustaining family life; (2) pervasive racial identification; and (3) education."

Boone proposes a domestic Marshall Plan—a comprehensive, integrated, experimental model to overhaul a large portion of one of the nation's major cities. The plan, a collaboration between public and private organizations, would carve out a large contiguous geographical and socioeconomic area of about 50,000 people in a city the size of Los Angeles or Chicago. This area would be an experimental laboratory in which to introduce innovative strategies, particularly in education, housing, and employment. A long-term commitment—as long as fifteen years—should, Boone believes, be built into this experiment. The program would involve on-site jobs and a new educational system not tied to the traditional system and to traditionally trained teachers. Instead, people would be recruited on the basis of their ability to be effective teachers.

"But the main thing is continuity," says Boone. "You've got fifteen years of commitment here to build this program so that young people can see that not only are they getting an education but they have an opportunity to build something of value." And concentrating the experiment on one area of one city in a holistic way—addressing all the pieces at once—can bring real results. Boone believes that the nation has the economic resources to undertake such an experiment but an absence of political will. The unresolved issue is how can such an experiment be undertaken in the absence of strong and powerful advocates?

Education has always been perceived by African Americans as the single most effective path to upward mobility. Acquiring an education is also linked to civil rights and civil liberties because of school segregation in the South previous to *Brown* v. *Board of Education* (1954). The issues confronting the new urban leaders are how to stem the tide of high school dropouts, provide a quality education, build new schools that are properly equipped for the technology era, and make schools safe.

Arlene Ackerman, superintendent of the San Francisco schools and former superintendent of the public schools in the District of Columbia from 1998 to 2000, says that the most critical problem facing urban school systems in poor communities is replacing worn-out school buildings.[13] In Washington, D.C., no new schools have been built in roughly thirty years, nor have the schools been well maintained. In 1997 a judge closed the schools until they could be repaired. The most competent urban school reformers cannot easily overcome these structural problems, upgrade the quality of instruction, and improve student outcomes unless citizens provide support.

Ackerman believes that citizens' confidence in public schools has eroded because of undue focus on issues other than children's education, such as teachers' pay, administrative problems, and school governance, leaving the children behind.

Lloyd Smith expresses frustration over the consequences of the movement of the black middle class out of the city: "The people who have kids in the schools are at a [low] socioeconomic level. They don't have the time or the interest [to be involved]. They don't give their children encouragement. When they are not educated themselves, they're not going to challenge any teacher." He feels that the presence of middle-class children in the classroom motivates poorer children to perform at a higher level.

"The fact is," says Ackerman, "that people who are articulate and educated, and who understand how to garner the resources and force the system to be accountable, are now in suburban schools working to make it happen there. Their voices are silent here in the urban schools. And silence almost means consent to those who are left." This silence is multiplied when the parents left behind are poor, have little formal education, and are burdened with a plethora of problems related to day-to-day living that make participating in their children's education difficult. Moreover, many parents are the products of urban schools themselves and did not fare well in the work world because of the shortcomings of their schooling. They have very poor skills and can neither articulate grievances against the schools nor advocate effectively on their children's behalf. Ackerman observes,

Although they want the same things that other parents want, they do not know how to navigate their way through the school, which can make them feel unwelcome and intimidate them so that, rather than go through that, they stay home. . . . The more educated and articulate you are, the more you know about the process, and the more you know that you can't trust the system, the more questions you ask, the more demands you are likely to make.

What are the remedies? A major step forward would be to educate disadvantaged parents to enable them to participate effectively in their children's education. This is especially important for language-minority parents who cannot communicate, for parents who do not have time to be involved, and for parents whose low educational level prevents them from understanding how they can make the schools deliver a more effective education.

A related issue is that traditionally black parents have deferred to teachers. This can probably be traced to the time when teachers held very high status in black communities, were respected as authority figures, and often resided in the same neighborhoods as the children they instructed. Ackerman observes:

Our parents didn't have to worry because the teachers were in our neighborhoods, they went to our churches, we saw them in the grocery stores. They reaffirmed the values. However, something has happened. This is probably not a popular thing to say, but in the process of integrating our schools we've lost that connectedness. . . . This connection is missing not only in the schools but also in the communities. We lived the same kind of experiences. We're not living through the same experiences now.

The low quality of public education is cited by Geoffrey Canada, director of Rheedlen Centers, a social service agency in New York City, as one of the two most critical urban problems (violence is the other). The schools "certainly failed my generation with the tracking system," he says. "But it has done

Geoffrey Canada

worse since then, which is hard to believe. There are [only] a few students from big inner-city schools who are going on and doing well in colleges and universities."[14] Since there is a scarcity of high-paying jobs that do not require postsecondary education, it is very difficult for young people in low-performing schools to get involved in the world of work. He agrees with Ackerman and Smith that the demographic mix of these communities and schools has changed for the worst. Canada remembers that

> there was [once] much more of a mix of communities. The public schools drew from several economic classes, the very poor, the poor, the not-so-poor, and those working- and middle-class families that were still part of the community. Even if individual blocks were segregated, the kids came into the schools. Now, what [later] happened . . . is that students were tracked. But when you look at economics you will find that most of the working-class and middle-class students were in the better classes and most of the very poor were in the classes that were tracked to not go to college. [There was not the same] mix inside the schools.

Further, when middle-income black families moved to suburbia they took with them not only their incomes and their influence but also their volunteered time. In effect, the Boy Scout master, the Girl Scout leader, the block captains, and the church leaders moved. Smith says that "those left are the very elderly, the very poor, and the very young. . . . Because of the flight of the middle class, there has been a demise in commercial activities and offerings—stores and other kinds of institutions. For instance, you could not come out here [to Marshall Heights] and find a basic store for sewing. You can't find a shoe repair shop. You can't find certain things out here." Commercial establishments follow the income groups that provide the largest profit margin, ensure safety, and provide a competent work force. Smith's concerns are based on his firsthand experiences attempting to stem the out-migration of middle-class individuals and families from his community. The out-migration from Marshall Heights in the District of Columbia has been to Prince George's County and, to a lesser extent, Montgomery County, both in nearby Maryland.

Another educational problem of the inner cities is the lack of alternatives to college, such as trade schools that provide students with marketable job skills. In the past, people could go directly from high school to industrial jobs that paid well and that offered job security and benefits. Canada notes that his mother would admonish him that if he did not finish high school he would "end up in the garment district, pushing one of those racks. And that was sort of considered to be a failure. Now, you can't end up anywhere if you don't have a good education, so that has really changed a lot."

Like Ackerman, Canada believes that the failure of the schools is caused by an overconcentration on issues of concern only to professional educators. Canada believes that professionals have been rewarded in spite of their failure to educate children, as schools give yearly raises to teachers and principals regardless of student performance. In New York City, as in many urban jurisdictions where teachers' unions are powerful, it is almost impossible for principals or teachers to be fired, no matter how poorly their students perform. Professionals are virtually immune from accountability for student outcomes.

That, he believes, is a mistake and has contributed to the erosion of standards for student success. It has also shifted blame for student performance from the professionals to the parents and the communities. Canada says,

> While these parents and the wider community bear some responsibility, it should be borne equally, and even more to a degree by the educational professionals. . . . No one told the professionals that they should treat the students differently because they are poor. If there were real levels of accountability, in that professional educators knew that they would have to bear certain negative consequences if the children they teach failed to learn, then we would see a lot more children performing at a higher level. If principals and teachers thought they would lose their jobs if children didn't learn, then the children would learn.

Some large urban school districts, including Chicago and Washington, D.C., have instituted accountability systems. In both cities, the superintendents or chief executive officers have fired principals at schools whose children had failing test scores. Each of these school systems also established an office of accountability. In Washington, the superintendent has gone a step further, implementing a system to fire teachers who, after a period of probation, fail to improve their teaching effectiveness.

Another issue of concern to urban public school systems is the growing use of vouchers and other forms of school choice. For example, through an act of the U.S. Congress, the District of Columbia can license up to twenty charter schools a year. Opponents of charter schools think these school compete with the larger public school system for funds, preventing a more rapid rebuilding program. Supporters argue that that is precisely what is intended: failing schools that are not doing their jobs should be challenged with competition from other schools.

The issue of school governance is also important. Several major school systems, including Chicago, Detroit, Washington, D.C., and Newark and Paterson, New Jersey, have abandoned the traditional system of elected school boards. The Illinois state legislature turned the Chicago schools over to the mayor of the city, who then appointed a board to handle oversight for the school system. The mayor of Detroit was also given the authority to appoint a school board. The District of Columbia's financial control board, which was established by the U.S. Congress in 1995 to eliminate the city's fiscal deficit, eliminated the powers of the elected school board and appointed a trustee board in 1997. A new hybrid board—four members representing the city's eight wards and four appointed by the mayor, along with a president elected at large by the citizens of Washington—took office in 2001.[15]

In summary, critics of the public school agree that society must review how it values education, not only kindergarten through grade twelve but adult education for immigrants and the poor as well. A systematic analysis is needed of how to prepare high school graduates to compete in the workplace, including a hard look at the achievement of such educational reforms as school choice and vouchers. As urban school systems continue to erode, municipalities will perhaps turn increasingly to appointed experts who can rise above partisan politics and use a holistic approach to solve the problems of funding, infrastructure, student retention, and training for the job market.

Violence and Poverty

Geoffrey Canada identifies violence as one of the most critical problems affecting poor urban communities. He also classifies violence as a public health issue, in accordance with the position taken by the U.S. Centers for Disease Control. In the New York City neighborhoods in which the Rheedlen Centers are located, violence has reached "epidemic proportions," according to Canada. "Violence is everywhere. . . . It occurs in schools and on the streets. . . . It impedes a young person's development in a very critical way. An interrelated problem is public safety. The threat to public safety in poor communities is enormous and is precipitated, in great measure, by drugs and violence."

At the nexus of all of these problems is poverty, which can be viewed as both a cause and a consequence. Poverty breeds violence, unsafe communities, and poor housing, poor medical care, and poor schools. The urban leaders' preoccupation with improving educational opportunity comes from their belief that it is the most likely solution to reducing poverty and eliminating violence. As Evelyn Moore, director of the National Child Development Institute in Washington, D.C. for the past thirty years, says:

> It is impossible to think of poverty [in all its dimensions] without thinking of education, because if you had an education you probably wouldn't be in poverty. At the core, the problem [of the urban poor] is race and poverty, and they get entangled, because some people appear to have transcended race . . . until the police stop them one night. Can you ever untangle race? Underneath it all is that of getting America past the race problem.[16]

Moore believes that race is at the bottom of the problem, followed by poverty, and then drugs, safety, violence, and teen pregnancy. When asked how society might alleviate these problems, Moore claims that the two most critical needs of children are good health and a good education. Because of her lifelong work as a child and family advocate, Moore's organization has devoted considerable resources to working on behalf of early childhood education programs.

> If I had to choose, I would choose health and education. I would integrate the two, because I don't think you can do one very well without the other. . . . This multitude of problems is unlike anything we have ever known about. And to some extent many of us are confused about how to get out of it. [These problems are] not something that was part of our lives, even when we were poor. . . . No one had to hit the floor [to avoid] bullets.

Moore thinks the government should help to ensure the safety of residents of violent urban neighborhoods. The high level of violence in Washington, D.C., she says, "is like there is no law and order. Police are shooting it out with each other at nightclubs. . . . This is like anarchy."

The new urban leaders tend to view violence as ever present, uncontrollable, spontaneous, and part of the fabric of the society—part of the culture of a generation of young men and women who grew up in its shadow. Older urban leaders, on the other hand, have for the most part not had personal experiences with violence, and their views differ from those of their younger colleagues. Stories of elderly women being robbed and beaten in front of supermarkets cause these older leaders to remember more peaceful times, when such behavior was anathema to all urban residents. They feel there should be strong sanctions against such behavior.

All of the leaders view violence as a symbol of the breakdown of the ties that hold communities together. One response has been to form organizations to provide role models for at-risk young black males in the hope that they can be steered away from antisocial behavior. Jeffrey Brown, cofounder of the Ten-Point Coalition, says that his group made the decision to take the church into the streets with the hope that those who were living and dying in the streets would come back into the church.[17] Since 1992, when the Ten-Point Coalition ministers first began walking the streets, talking to gang members, and persuading them to lay down their weapons, they have helped to lower the rate of violence. Brown says,

> There are some 265 unsolved murders in Boston, and most of them are black-on-black murders. Based on that, there are about 240 families still grieving over who shot their son, daughter, uncle or father, or brother. . . . Yes, we do have racism and all these challenges. But it is hard for me to talk about racism when I'm trying to get the gun out of the hand of a black kid who has shot another kid. . . . The only way we can deal with demons like racism is to clean up these problems of unsolved murders. We've got to show that we're strong on the inside through rebuilding our communities before we focus entirely on racism on the outside.

The tough issues that the most at-risk populations of blacks face are, ironically, related to the role of the black middle class and the black intelligentsia, both of whom are criticized by Eugene Rivers for not playing the important role they should in fixing these problems.

Robert Woodson is the most vociferous critic of the black middle class for failing to help solve the problems of the black underclass. Woodson achieved national renown for building leadership capacity among public housing residents and eliminating violence among warring drug dealers in a Washington, D.C., housing project. He is founder and president of the National Center for Neighborhood Enterprise, an organization that works with urban dwellers whom others have given up on. An outspoken critic of what he calls the "poverty industry," he attacks black leaders for being more interested in maintaining their privileged status than in helping to make the poor self-sufficient.

Ten or twenty years ago, when the devastation and self-destruction was first evidenced in urban areas, experts equipped with "population profiles" assumed that the root of the problem lay in racism and poverty. On this premise, trillions of dollars were channeled through the bureaucracies of antipoverty programs, and the issue of race gave birth to a virtual industry, spawning the careers of authors, speakers, and a spectrum of specialists. Meanwhile, conditions in the inner city continued to worsen, and a prescient Daniel Patrick Moynihan predicted that it would only be a matter of time before the crisis permeated all levels of society. Moynihan was right.[18]

Woodson's position draws criticism from those who view him as a politically conservative leader interested in appealing to white conservatives. Woodson is unflappable in the face of such criticism. In fact, he appears to thrive on being on the offensive against his detractors. He has been central in establishing the framework for a critical debate on the causes of, the consequences of, and the solutions to the problems affecting the urban underclass. In his 1998 book, he asks,

Why haven't we heard more about these modern-day Josephs? Why isn't their success common knowledge? Why hasn't their great potential to address not only the needs of the underclass but the problems that exist among every race, ethnicity, and income bracket [been used]? There are many powerful social, economic, and political institutions that have a proprietary interest in continued existence of the problems of the poor.[19]

Even though it is difficult to agree with Woodson's view that there is a sinister plan to "keep poverty in its place for profit," his argument raises the important question of whether the most effective methods are being used to solve the problems of the poor. It is unlikely that most people employed in what Woodson refers to as the poverty industry are willfully preventing the poor from acquiring a better education, better housing, and better health care. These may be unintended consequences of these workers' inaction, incompetence, or lack of creativity. According to Woodson, the interest groups include members of the civil rights establishment, a massive poverty industry that owes its existence to the problems of the poor, and the politicians aligned with them. To these experts, the poor represent a $340 billion commodity, in terms of annual allotments to federal and state programs that have been instituted in their name.[20]

Woodson argues that the educated, articulate leaders who serve in mediator roles for the urban poor are no longer needed because the poor can speak for themselves. He believes these "gatekeepers" stand between the poor and funding agencies, for example, and should be removed. Toward this end, Woodson devotes considerable time and effort to developing grassroots leadership through training programs and forums to teach the poor to represent their own communities. It is here that his criticism of people who work in the so-called poverty industry is sharpest, because the "established institutions that have a vested interest in the continuance and expansion of funding the 'poverty and race industries' have formed a virtual iron triangle that has blocked the message that solutions to the most critical problems of the poor already exist and they are to be found, not among the credentialed, professional experts, but in the neighborhoods that suffer the problems."[21]

Few of these "mediator-leaders," says Woodson, try to help the black underclass to be upwardly mobile because it has not been in their interest to work themselves out of their jobs. He feels that the successes of his organization in nurturing grassroots leaders are rarely publicized by this establishment because many of his organization's grassroots leaders are poor people whose prior experiences fall outside that of conventional behavior: some of his greatest successes, for example, have been with those who work with, or are themselves, ex-convicts, violent offenders, including gang members, and recovering addicts—individuals who do not engender the same level of empathy as those who have lived within the boundaries of conventional standards.

The mission of the National Center for Neighborhood Enterprise is to develop leadership capacity to work with a population that has few advocates. The clergy and other civil societies, he says, have to start to "love, lecture, discipline, and defend these kids like they're their own." To address disorganization, he calls for postintegration-era leaders who are young, God-fearing, and not afraid to get their hands dirty—leaders who will press for economic and cultural literacy. Woodson goes so far as to say that many social welfare workers, whom he refers to as "poverty pimps," are the chief beneficiaries of large agency budgets. He praises the efforts of groups like the Alliance of Black Men, which mentors former gang members. "When I see that people like the members of the Alliance of Black Men, who are making effective change in people's lives, don't have jobs or housing or the things that we associate with social programs, I ask myself, Why did these young men stop their tough fighting? It was not because the alliance said I will give you a job. No. It is because these men were examples of moral excellence."

Implementing the Vision: Two Stories

Jeffrey Brown describes in chapter 5 the traumatic incidents involving the teenage gang members in his neighborhood that set him on a path to discovering his true mission. His special religious calling would not be to build a suburban megachurch but rather to tackle the problems of gang violence, domestic violence, poverty, hunger, and drug abuse.

After he made his choice, he invited a woman from the Alliance against Drugs to speak at his church. "She said some things that chilled me," he recalls. "One thing she said was that this is a lost generation because of its violence, and we need to abandon it because there is nothing we can do. We shouldn't expend our efforts on saving them. We should concentrate more on the next generation coming behind them."

He could not understand how others could give up on a whole generation. Because of his vocation, especially, he believes in the power of redemption. If sinners can be saved, then why not these children? Two incidents—the killing of Jessie McKie and this woman's statement—hardened Brown's resolve to take his message to community residents and to find ways to save the children that the Alliance Against Violence said could not be helped. This is, in effect, when he became an avowed community leader with a specific focus. The next stage for him was to design a plan of action.

Brown gave up on his doctoral studies at Harvard and volunteered at Cambridge Ridge and Latin School, in the student service center for school clubs. Brown quickly realized that, although he was making an important contribution to these young people, those who needed help had already dropped out of school. Most were on the streets engaged in antisocial activities.

> I had to go to Columbia and the public parks where they were hanging out. That is where I needed to go to reach those kids. The great thing about being at the high school is that I knew all the players. If I was able to make an impact in the high school, I had to reach the kids on the streets, because the high school students had a fear and respect for the gang members. I started walking the streets, but I wasn't sure what to do. I just knew I had to do something.[22]

During this period Brown met Eugene Rivers, of the Dorchester community, Ray Hammond, of the Jamaica community, and Bruce Wall, of the Roxbury area. These clergy, like Brown, had organized their own communities, and Rivers and

Hammond had already held a rally at a crack house to symbolize the seriousness of the drug problem in the community. When the Morning Star incident occurred (see chapter 4), some of the local ministers arranged for the gang to apologize to John Borders, the pastor of the church. Borders discovered that two of the gang members were also members of his church. This small nucleus of ministers—Jeffrey Brown, Gene Rivers, John Borders, and Ray Hammond—realized they had to mobilize the community to fight the gang problem, and Rivers issued an invitation to the community to meet at his house on the following Friday night. About a dozen people came.

Beginning in July 1992, each weekend night around ten o'clock the clergymen began their walks through the tough streets controlled by the gangs. They were not sure why they were out there; neither was the public. They were not police officers, nor were they drug users or dealers. Gang members were fascinated by this band of clergy but refused to have prolonged conversations with them. They were watching, trying to determine who they were, what they were doing, and whether they were motivated by what they could get out of it. Brown says, "They wanted to see if we were serious in doing this and that we were not doing it for self-profit but for greater good."

These clergy continued to walk the streets until their presence began to take effect. Violence on the streets of Boston declined precipitously, and a truce was called among warring gangs. From these grassroots efforts, the organization called the Ten-Point Coalition was founded. In time, other cities would adopt the Ten-Point Coalition's strategy for dealing with violence in their communities.

If Geoffrey Canada has a mission, it is to find ways to help single mothers with young children get out of poverty and take care of their basic needs—housing, education, health care, jobs, safety. Canada was awarded the Heinz Prize in 1988 for his work with poor children and families.

Canada's interest in youth issues began during his own youth, when he was deprived of the security, love, and comfort of a two-parent household. He began to mentor children when he was an adolescent, demonstrating an unusually early sensitivity to the plight of poor children. His single-minded interest in saving children from their unsafe environments by attempting to reach each child in the neighborhoods that the Rheedlen Centers and the Beacon Schools serve can be emulated by other child welfare advocates. "I grew up in an impoverished community [in New York City]," he says. "And insofar as economics and social issues are concerned, I saw lots of these problems firsthand. It was very clear to me that this is a country that offers great promise if the ideals of the country, such as equal access and equal opportunity, are realized. That means that there must be a level playing field for all children." The two most pressing issues in Canada's work with the poor are eliminating violence and improving education. He is one of the most devoted and powerful advocates against violence—domestic violence, gang violence, street violence, school violence—in poor urban neighborhoods.

Diminishing federal support has meant increasing numbers of needy families seeking help from private agencies like the Rheedlen Centers, placing an extraordinary burden on such private agencies. For the centers to be effective under these circumstances, they had to shift their focus from direct intervention to working with schools, churches, housing authorities, block associations, tenant groups, businesses, and political and social clubs in the neighborhoods where the families live. It is Canada's belief that mutually dependent institutions are more effective in providing services to the needy.

Rheedlen operates twelve sites throughout New York City, mostly in Harlem and the Bronx. When the agency shifted its focus from the family to the neighborhood, it expanded its points of intervention to include these other institutions, with the assumption that the agency now serves not just families but neighborhoods. A program called the Harlem Children's Zone Initiative is an example of this new philosophy. It functions in a twenty-four-block area in Central Harlem (from 116th Street to 123d Street and from Fifth Avenue to Eighth Avenue) and is divided into four minizones. The neighborhood has been reorganized so that there is a working relationship between the preschools and the tenant and block associations, with the objective of tracking each child from birth to three years old and linking each child with a caring adult. "We are trying to rebuild communities in a very pragmatic way," says Canada. The challenges are enormous, but Canada is optimistic.[23]

Has the community intervention approach been successful? "It's too early to measure the success, but we have seen a couple of things which indicate to us that we are on the right track." The centers have "seen a willingness on the part of community residents to come together to set priorities, to work jointly on those priorities, and to . . . tackle some of the more difficult, long-term issues: drugs, crime, employment of parents, and failing schools." This suggests that if these efforts are sustained and nourished they will prosper. Canada has set the next seven years as the time frame for successful development.

When asked how the program's effectiveness will be evaluated, Canada says, "There are some things that measure success which are different than if you were to talk to an evaluator or a policymaker. I consider our work successful when the children have the same opportunities in our communities that they have in other communities," a measure that lacks the rigor of professional program evaluators. When asked to explain this inconsistency, Canada says, "People have a hard time with [my view] because I want our children to have access to dance and music classes and sports, recreational, cultural, academic, and health programs. To have access to them, to me, is a real measure of success."

Canada was reminded that the availability of a broad range of programs alone does not ensure that they would be on par with those in economically advantaged neighborhoods. His response is that the issues of access, program quality, and participant usage is important.

The shame of this is that we're starting with the basics of just having these programs exist. There is no way that you are going to have success if you only have two programs and don't have the other thirty that make up the menu of opportunities that children and families need. We know what works. Look at communities that are functioning, and you can see very clearly what works.

Which of the many programs he operates does he hold up as a model? The closest examples are the Harlem Children's Home and Beacon Schools, which operate as community centers. They are open seven days a week, twelve hours a day, every day of the year. Funded through the New York City Department of Youth and Community Development, they provide a menu of supportive services for children, adolescents, young adults, and adults. Rheedlen operates one of the fifty Beacon Schools in existence.

Canada attributes the success of this particular Beacon School to its creative approach to serving young people. The school operates out of Public School 194, at a cost of about

$450,000 a year. Its mission is not just to serve children but also to serve the community. Moreover, it does not focus solely on serving individuals who have problems but also provides a resource to all community residents. The Beacon School exists without stigma: individuals visit the school to socialize, to hold community meetings, and to engage in various forms of community building. At the same time, however, the social services exist for drug or alcohol abuse treatment, counseling, and similar needs. This is a model for restoring or rebuilding community through the involvement of individuals and civil society organizations.

Beacon Schools use one of the "chief fundamental structures in communities, which are the schools. Schools exist in every poor community," Canada says. "The Beacon Schools serve hundreds of young people and adults on a regular basis within a facility that was paid for with tax dollars. I think it is our best approach." Beacon Schools are located in middle-class, working-class, and poor communities. They become the hub of the community and serve as community centers. Canada summarizes his views:

> Our kids need drug treatment, help with juvenile justice issues, and education. They also need a plethora of positive activities that all kids need to keep them from getting into trouble. This is not an issue as to whether you engage in prevention before trouble occurs, or intervention after it occurs. You have to do both all the time. The more prevention you do, the less intervention will be needed. The most serious problem is that there [are] inadequate . . . services for children.

While Canada is an optimistic, passionate advocate, he is equally the pragmatic leader. He contends that most of the problems his agency deals with are solvable, given the proper resources. When asked what motivates him to be the powerful advocate that he is, he explains,

It is the work itself. I think that we as a nation are at a crossroads. We have choices to make about what kind of country we're going to be. Are we going to be a country that gives lip service to [child welfare] while we embrace horrible realities by the way we operate? This country talks about freedom, yet we have plagues. We talk about equality, and we have denied women and other people their equal rights. It is lip service to an ideal, which makes hypocrites.

CHAPTER SEVEN

PROMISING PRACTICES: FOUR CASE STUDIES

Despite the obstacles the new urban leaders face, there are some success stories that give great reason for optimism. The four case studies described below were designed to have a long-term impact and to produce systemic change. They include a program to detoxify pregnant women so they can deliver drug-free babies and acquire marketable skills; two schools—one private and one public—whose students live in economically distressed high-risk neighborhoods but who score above the national norm on standardized tests; and a gardening project.

The Providence–Saint Mel Independent School

Paul Adams, the president of Providence–Saint Mel independent school for over a quarter century, is a big man with big ideas. He is in the mold of the strict, old-fashioned schoolmaster who is so grounded in his philosophy that there is scant difference between his professional and personal lives. "I believe in children," he says. "I believe specifically that inner-city children should have as much a right to slices of the American pie as anybody else."[1] An essential part of Adams's mission is to prove to a skeptical public that low-

Paul Adams

income minority children can excel in education at a level equal to their middle-class peers.

> I'm so tired of hearing about what inner-city children can't do. Part of my success has been to [demonstrate] that it can be done. Competent teachers are critical to the school's success. Another source of my success comes from a strong board of directors to raise the money that we need to run the school. I believe that you can take what you have and make it work if people are competent in their areas and have the same goals. [Then] we can take on the world. We offer an opportunity for people to save a child's life.

Paul Adams rescued Providence-Saint Mel—often referred to as the "school that refused to die"—in 1978 when the Catholic Archdiocese of Chicago decided to close it. Launching a national campaign seeking donations to help him keep the school open, he eventually was able to purchase the structure from the religious order and turn it into a private school.

A key component of Adams's educational philosophy is the belief that exposing students to the world beyond their immediate environment allows them to gain self-confidence and to develop the ability to adapt to other cultures without feelings of isolation or inferiority. Saint Mel students can participate as early as third grade in music and art summer camps as well as in college programs at universities such as Cornell, Harvard, and Stanford. These students are primarily kids who do well in school and who "would be able to withstand the environment that they're going to, because most of the time, they're going to be the only black kids in the program. If they have problems about [integrating with] white folks, you're going to be wasting a lot of time and energy and end up ruining the opportunity for someone else." Highly structured tutorials are provided to enhance student performance: students may have two hours of tutoring and study time in their school day and an additional tutoring session during the weekend.

Adams's method has paid off. In 1978, 296 students were enrolled in Saint Mel; today there are about 700. Seniors' scores on the ACT (American College Testing program) match the statewide average and exceed the average for Chicago public schools. The Scholastic Achievement Test is given to top students, and their scores exceed the national average. The college acceptance rate for Saint Mel seniors is 100 percent. Between 1978 and 1988, 95 percent of Saint Mel graduates went to college; this ratio rose to 98 percent between 1988 and 1998. Traditionally, Saint Mel has served the children of Garfield Park's poorest families. Today there is greater diversity among the students, with children from middle-income families and neighborhoods also attending. The school still strives, however, to remain close to its mission of serving the children whose families are least able to afford a high-quality education.

How does Saint Mel create and maintain its high level of success? What are the reinforcing factors ensuring the maintenance of a system in which students conform to the rules and regulations, where excellence is demanded, and where high expectations are usually fulfilled? How does Adams motivate students to come to school long before the 8:00 a.m. starting time and to stay late for extra tutoring?

The two essential ingredients for success, according to Adams, are discipline and competent teachers. Standards of conduct are high and inflexible. Students are required, for example, to adhere to a strict dress code. They cannot wear baggy pants, sunglasses, biker pants, or tank tops. Boys are not allowed to wear earrings, and although students may carve designs in their hair, they cannot wear overly revealing or tight clothing. Students are fined $10 if they are tardy for class five times and $15 for walking on the school's lawn. When asked how he exerts discipline, Adams quickly replies,

> Right away. We have a discipline code and a dean of students who has worked for me for twenty-seven years. When children become discipline problems, we have them come to work on Saturdays. They come for eight hours. It's amazing how well that works. I don't believe in taking kids out of class and sending them home for three or four days. If I send you home, it's for good.

Teachers respond to all possible early warning signs to determine whether a student is headed for trouble. Intervention occurs at virtually all levels. Parents are required to meet certain expectations, including paying the annual tuition and becoming partners in their children's education. They are strongly encouraged to visit the school often and to attend a minimum of four progress-report meetings. The progress report occurs four weeks before grades are released. Adams does not think it is "necessary to have a progress report when your grades already have been determined. If they [the parents] don't show up, we make them pay a $25 fine."

Adams operates the school without even a secretary. His proprietary attitude toward his school is demonstrated in every area, from planting the grass to chasing away drug dealers to expelling students who use drugs. Students who disagree with his rules of strict conduct are asked to leave. Adams does not waste time on those who do not wish to conform to the requirements of his program—there are too many applicants on the waiting list.

Early on, Adams realized that he not only had to control the environment inside the school but also the environment around the school. The economic blight—poor housing, poverty, and unemployment—was glaring. "Frankly, I think that's a natural extension of institutions within communities," he explains. "They should have a positive effect on the community. Education in the inner city has been too abstract, and what I wanted to do was base the education in reality so the kids could actually see that with education you could do certain things."

Adams and his board organized a development corporation and built twenty-six rental townhouses in the school's neighborhood. The housing units serve as a tax credit for the school and should eventually become a revenue producer. The housing was built with a nominal amount of capital. "Most things we do, we start without money. We have been 'land banking' recently, and I think that within the next two [or] three months we should have some fifty lots that we can put together and decide what kind of housing will be constructed." The group is also remodeling a building for condominiums. The added benefit of Adams's economic development is that some of his students and their families now live in housing provided by the school. The nonprofit corporation that operates Saint Mel also runs a McDonald's restaurant that serves the surrounding neighborhood. Students are employed, and half of the profits go to the school.

Ten years ago Providence–Saint Mel began to offer a summer enrichment program called SOAL—Summer Opportunities of a Lifetime. It was designed to expose students to other cultures and institutions across the United States and abroad. Each summer a hundred Saint Mel students spend a month at boarding schools such as Phillips Exeter and Choate on the

East Coast or at universities such as Harvard, Oxford, and the University of Paris. Other students participate in Outward Bound, which teaches survival and leadership skills in the wilderness; others intern at Chicago-area businesses. United Airlines subsidizes the cost of students' international travel. The exchange schools and other participants often cover tuition and expenses or reduce their usual rates.

Adams's educational philosophy, which is embodied in the school's mission statement and recited each day before classes start, states that students must "dream" but that they must also "earn the right to dream." Students are thus reminded every day that they must work hard and not expect to be given grades or opportunities they did not earn. Adams's job is to translate the abstract concepts of high expectations into concrete reality. He does this, for example, by refunding the tuition of students who receive straight As, honoring high-achieving students in special assemblies, and providing opportunities for these students to travel and study in other parts of the country and abroad. This combination of rewards and punishments seems to have struck the proper balance to achieve success.

Adams has not achieved these successes alone. He has built a strong core of teachers and counselor who adhere to the basic elements of his model of success. "We tell [the teachers], 'These are the things that we know work. We would like you to follow through on that, and if you have a suggestion for doing it better, talk to us before you start implementation.' We tell people that if they're going to work here, please support [the curriculum]; if not, go somewhere else." One of Adams's major concerns, however, is teacher turnover, caused by the noncompetitive salaries that Saint Mel offers—roughly two-thirds of the pay for teachers in Chicago public schools. The school has an operating budget of $5 million, of which about $3 million has to be raised. The school's board of directors consists of some of Chicago's corporate titans as well as local foundations. Prominent supporters of the school include Oprah Winfrey (who gave the school $1 million) and entrepreneur Stedman Graham, who is a member of the school's board of directors. In spite of this support, the funding cannot support high teacher pay.

Providence–Saint Mel is one of a growing number of private schools located in inner-city neighborhoods that are viewed as an alternative to problem-ridden public schools. It stands as a model for the increasing numbers of such schools across the nation that are alternatives to poor-performing public schools. Parent advocates view these schools as a way to recreate the type of educational environment they experienced, before the public schools became rife with problems. An essential feature for them is discipline and high performance standards, watchwords at Providence–Saint Mel.

The Houston Unified Charter School District

Urban school reformers have not been very successful in transforming inner-city public schools into effective learning environments, on par with schools in middle-class communities. Thus alternatives—charter schools and access to schools outside the neighborhood—have gained popularity. Some people view charter schools, however, as a threat to the public school system: since they are usually small, they are able to offer smaller class sizes than the mainstream public schools; and since many charter school leaders think "outside the box," there is the perception that these schools serve an elite group of students. Charter schools are not, however, always battlegrounds for public school administrators and innovators. In the best scenario, charter schools serve as fertile ground for public school educators and administrators to experiment with new techniques and curricula. The ideal charter school is one whose goals are supported by public school personnel and in which public and charter school administrators work together.

One of the most effective programs in which public and charter school personnel cooperate is the Houston Unified Charter School District.[2] Superintendent Thaddeus Lott led this experiment in urban education within the public school system. Lott was formerly principal of Wesley Elementary School in the Acres Homes section of Houston. Wesley Elementary had all the flaws of a very poorly performing public school: in 1975 only 18 percent of its third graders were scoring at grade level in reading on the Iowa Basic Skills Tests. By 1980, through the efforts of its principal, 85 percent of the students scored at or above grade level, reaching 100 percent in 1996. Statewide, only 70 percent of third graders in schools with similar demographic characteristics had passing scores. The superior performance of the students at Wesley led parents in Acres Home to ask the Houston school board to allow Lott to take over three additional schools. In 1995 the board approved the formation of a separate charter school system. Throughout the process, he received strong support from Houston School Superintendent Rodney Paige, now secretary of the U.S. Department of Education.

Four schools—three elementary schools and one middle school—form the Houston Unified Charter School System. The students live in the neighborhoods in which the schools are located. This demonstrates that it is possible to operate high-quality schools for poor children in their own neighborhoods without bolstering the enrollment with middle-class students from other neighborhoods.

Successful leaders first transform an organization to meet certain criteria, then ensure its continued success by setting high standards for others, demanding excellence from their primary constituents, and implementing rules that allow them to remove or minimize the disruption of those who do not comply. Lott's leadership embodies these characteristics and more. He is very clear about his goals and objectives and the methods he uses to achieve them. He advocates a back-to-basics approach but also believes that reforms must consider the whole child, including the family and the community. In this context, Lott has identified impoverished single-parent families as the single most-pressing problem in the neighborhood served by the charter schools he administers. Many of the children enrolled in these schools are being reared by grandparents or other relatives, because the children's parents do not have the stable lives—including jobs and wages—necessary to support their children.

Lott is deeply concerned about the difficult challenges that await such children and is constantly trying to find new strategies to level the playing field for them so they can compete with children from anywhere in the nation. Lott's philosophy, on which he bases his curriculum, thus mandates that children be taught basic skills as soon as possible. Kindergartners, for example, are taught basic reading skills as soon as they enter school, enabling them to compete with their peers in Houston's middle-class school districts. Lott contends that these children must be taught to read in kindergarten, otherwise they will lag behind. They enter school with disadvantages that must be tackled and overcome as quickly as possible. Learning to read, for Lott, is fundamental to students' acquiring good writing skills, understanding good literature, thinking critically and analytically, and ultimately having the skills to compete in a technologically driven society.

Lott's philosophy is also manifested by the way he relates to and interacts with his teachers. Lott sets very high standards and expects his teachers to adhere to strict guidelines. Failure to do so results in dismissal. At any given time, he or his assistant—a master teacher—may visit a classroom unannounced. Teaching methods and other classroom behavior is subject to questioning, instruction, and revision on the spot. These corrective actions are part of Lott's ongoing teacher education and training. Teachers who do not adapt either leave voluntarily or are asked to leave. There is little room for teachers to experiment with their own teaching styles, because Lott does not feel it necessary to veer from DISTAR (Direct Instructional System for Teaching and Remediation, now called Reading Mastery and Connecting Math Concepts), the method he uses in the charter schools.

Lott tries "to find teachers who, to some extent, can already see the problem. They can already identify with the need," he says, because they "are visionaries and can extend themselves into the future. Based on what they see, they can predict what [the outcomes] are going to look like." Lott and several lead teachers are engaged in the arduous task of reforming a poorly performing middle school. "It is exciting," he says, "to work with a highly competent team—throughout the summer and whenever necessary, without having to watch the clock—experimenting with various strategies and scenarios and trying to place the students academically." Intensive diagnosis and grouping of students help ensure that, when they begin school in the fall, they will be given the tools they need to acquire a firm educational foundation. Other parts of laying the groundwork are identifying the appropriate instructional materials and intensively training teachers in the use of these materials.

But the main factor in the success of these schools seems to be Lott himself. "You can walk into a classroom," he says, "and after five minutes . . . see what's wrong." Because of his deep familiarity with the curriculum, he and the teachers are then able to take corrective actions immediately. Lott's passion is to teach teachers how to do their jobs well.

Lott's best assurance that he is on the right track is his students' high standardized test scores. On the Stanford 9 (Stanford Achievement Test Series, ninth edition, the classic standardized test given to students from first grade through twelfth grade), his first graders test at the eighty-second percentile, "which means we did one hell of a job teaching them how to read in kindergarten." The Stanford 9, a national norm-tested exam, is given toward the end of the school year in order to judge a student's performance and how a particular school is operating in comparison with others. Lott is one of the few superintendents to also give the test to kindergarten students. His are the only urban schools that rank among the top ten or eleven schools in the Houston Independent School District.

One reason Lott's program works is that it depends on a highly specialized system of diagnostic and placement criteria. The rate at which students master skills differs over time and among children. "If you don't teach a child at his instructional level, you will teach him at his frustration level," Lott says. A child may be a slow learner, but that does not necessarily mean he or she belongs in special education. Only 3 percent of the students enrolled in Lott's elementary schools are in special education, compared to 10 percent for the rest of Houston's elementary schools. (Comparable data for the District of Columbia for the school year 1996–97 indicate that the percentage of children aged six through twenty-one being served under the Individuals with Disabilities Education Act was 7.01 percent. The national average for the same year was 8.62 percent.)

Lott initiated an experimental program in 1985 that entails year-round education in eleven pilot schools of the Houston Unified Charter School District. Children were placed in one of four groups, and children who performed significantly below expectations were asked to attend two twenty-day sessions. This program produced enormously positive results in student achievement.

> We actually got the parents to commit to sending the low-performing children to two intersessions, as we called it, and they had one intersession off. The high-performing kids could do the same, but theirs was more for enrichment. The lower and middle kids zoomed. We got more out of that [intersession program] than anything that I have ever done because we made sure the teachers were outstanding teachers. It was just not a time when they [the children] came in [to school] and played.

Lott's philosophy on differences in pace of learning runs counter to the prevailing educational philosophy. His belief is that many children placed in special education classes do not belong there, that such children simply learn at a slower pace and need to be able to move at their own rate. They need to be taught how to master the material in the same manner as faster learners are taught. The only difference should be that these children are taught at a slower pace.

The success of Lott's reform also rests on positive parental involvement, including such direct participation in the affairs of the school as volunteering in the classroom, chaperoning field trips, and fund-raising. Again, Lott departs from convention by defining the role of parents in narrow terms. "What we require of parents is one word—support." And although he expects parents to take responsibility for the education of their children, the major responsibility for outcomes rests with Lott and his teachers. The key to a successful relationship between parents and the school, says Lott, is to establish lines of communication and develop a partnership to convey to children the importance of education. In addition to four formal advisory meetings a year between teachers and parents, parents and teachers talk on the phone as often as necessary, sometimes daily.

Lott recognizes that there are barriers to effective learning over which he has little control. He identifies these barriers as "mobility" and "standards." As to mobility, parents might move the child out of the school system if they feel that the curriculum is too rigorous or if their child's grades are too low. Some parents move their children from one school to another in search of the elusive "perfect education" or the ideal school, only to find that it does not exist. These parents usually bring their children back to Lott's schools because they find that higher grades do not necessarily mean that their child is learning more. Mobility is directly related to the absence of national education standards: there is no single set of standards that teachers must meet, no single set of expectations that parents agree to, and no explicit body of knowledge that children must learn. Standards would encourage, if not require, teacher, administrator, and parent accountability. Children would master prerequisites before they advanced to the next grade, thereby remedying the problem of social promotion, which plagues many large urban school systems. Lott believes that many nonreaders are promoted on to graduation simply because we lack national standards.

It is impossible to separate Lott's background and personal philosophy from the way the schools' programs are structured. The hiring of personnel, the selection of a curriculum, the intensive on-site and continuous teacher training, the expectations of parental support, and the students' mastery of specific skills are built into Lott's system.

Lott's philosophy of educational reform is both simple and complex. It is simple in the sense that Lott assumes that all children can learn in the proper environment and that children must be taught in a benevolent yet strict matter. There is also, however, a highly complex system of interdependent parts that are synchronized to work together. What one finds in Lott is a strong independent-minded leader who is willing to go against convention. He has adopted "direct instruction" as a teaching methodology at a time when others have abandoned it. He expresses little concern for critics who view his approach as autocratic and stiffening. The results in student outcomes have proven his method a stunning success. Although Lott, in the vernacular, "runs a tight ship," his methods have been standardized and can be replicated. Thus Lott's work is an example of sustainable social change at its best. Lott has developed a systematic approach to problem solving, undergirds this approach with strict guidelines, and maintains high expectations for his own and others' performance.

Lott's tenure at the Houston Independent School District has not been without controversy. Critics compare the school to a military boot camp. Children fold their arms across their chests when they walk down the halls and, at times, when they shout out drills. The program's concept is "practice makes perfect." Many of Lott's critics are associated with the whole language movement, which holds that word recognition skills are acquired by students in the context of reading and writing, that children learn to read by being offered rich pictures and text, and that students need immersion experiences by considering a variety of meanings. This approach is the opposite of the direct instruction advocated by Lott, in which children are systematically taught specific writing and reading skills. Lott believes that the children in his schools need the type of education in which basic educational skills are acquired through teachers explaining the skills that the students need to master and using certain methods to achieve them. The teachers provide help as needed.

The drudgery of drills has led to teacher turnover as well. A fifth of Lott's faculty—more than twice the district's average—are in their first year of teaching. This may be the result of the demands made on the teaching staff, especially the responsibility for their students' test scores. Teachers are also subject to constant oversight by master teachers. Some may well view this as intrusive, but Lott thinks it contributes to the success of his program. Finally, there is the controversy over standardized tests. Critics assert that teachers must teach to the test rather than allowing children's creativity and natural learning to blossom.

In sum, Thaddeus Lott has proven that poor inner-city children can learn at the same level as children in Houston's most elite public schools. Although his style has been called autocratic and is viewed by some liberal educators as intrusive, he has dared to do something very few educational leaders have done: place the major responsibility for a child's learning on the teachers and, ultimately, on himself. He appears to care little for what the critics say about him, emphasizing that, in the final analysis, the only thing that matters is the children's success.

The Haymarket Center's Maternal Addiction Program

Many of the new urban leaders face extremely difficult challenges because they work with people whose families and friends have given up on them and who have taxed the resources of formal institutions to their limit. Susan Flynn, director of the Maternal Addiction Program at Chicago's Haymarket Center, has designed a program for some of the most troubled individuals in Chicago: pregnant women who are addicted to drugs.[3] Many of these women already have children, and the treatment center is their last hope. If they follow the rules and regulations and work hard, they can join the large number of women who have preceded them in overcoming their drug habit and giving birth to drug-free infants. If they go the extra step, they may also be released with jobs, housing, and a renewed sense of self-esteem.

Flynn was trained as a psychiatric social worker. Like many social workers, she realized that her formal training was ineffective in dealing with clients with multiple needs. Flynn says,

A lot of our clients came in not only with psychiatric symptoms but also with symptoms of substance abuse, addiction, and dependence. Traditionally, substance abuse and mental health services are polarized, so in a psychiatric hospital you would treat the psychiatric symptoms but wouldn't touch the substance abuse. And we saw these clients come back into our system repeatedly. At that point, I realized that if we're going to be successful with these clients we need to treat both disorders. . . . I became interested in the field of addiction. I came to Haymarket about two and a half years ago to focus, again more specifically, on addiction.

The Haymarket Center, located in Chicago's old Skid Row area, was founded in 1975 by James West (now medical director at the Betty Ford Clinic) and Father Ignatius McDermott, a Catholic priest. Over time, Haymarket began to serve a broader clientele, including women and those addicted to substances besides alcohol. The center started the Maternal Addiction Program in the early 1990s; it was one of some fifty federally funded demonstration projects in the United States. The program has thirty-two beds for pregnant women eighteen years and older who suffer from substance addiction (most of them range in age from twenty-four to thirty-two). Women can enter the program at any point during their pregnancy and are required to stay until they deliver their babies. Since the program began, 400 drug-free babies have been delivered.

Haymarket was initially given funding to work with women who already had given birth, an approach that Father McDermott did not agree with. "Why would we wait until the damage is done?" he asked. "We'd really like to treat these women during their pregnancies so we can ensure a healthy delivery." The program experienced problems with funding because pregnant addicted women pose enormous legal risks for health care and social service providers: babies born to addicted mothers have a high risk of developing physical and cognitive deficits and of being exposed to the HIV virus and other sexually transmitted diseases.

The women who enter the Maternal Addiction Program are at the highest end of the risk scale because they are current drug users. The admission policy is to accept all applicants if possible, but greater weight is given to current or active drug users. Once admitted, the women are detoxified, given maternal health care, and taught parenting skills. After they deliver their babies, even normal maternal duties can be very stressful to mothers recovering from addiction, since most of these women have never parented while sober. A major part of the program focuses on helping mothers cope with normal maternal responsibilities. Staff members also assess the vocational and educational needs of their clients, linking them with social service providers who can help them complete their education or get jobs. In addition, the program involves family members as much as possible. Flynn says,

We encourage family support, for we understand that you cannot treat substance abuse in a vacuum. Eventually, these clients are going back into various social systems, whether it is the school, family, or all the different things that were in place before they came to Haymarket. We certainly want to include the family; we want to teach them about addiction. Many times, family members become mystified by the recovery process. They hear a new lingo being spoken, and the client has new friends. The twelve-step slogans that they hear can be intimidating. . . . Therefore, we want to educate the family members on the process of recovery and the disease of addiction. We want [them to look] at addiction as a family disease. It affects everybody, not just the person who has the addiction; everybody needs to recover. We want to keep them as involved as possible so that [the women] have support as they go through the process.

The program allows women with children at home to bring one or two toddlers with them during treatment, on the premise that not only the mothers but the children too are in need of treatment. This integrated approach recognizes that drug addiction wreaks havoc on the entire family and that patients need to be treated as part of the extended family.

An on-site clinic offering prenatal care was opened recently by Sinai Family Health Systems in conjunction with the program at Haymarket. Before this relationship was developed, women were sent to the county hospital for medical attention, causing them to miss a full day of treatment. Further, the county hospital is located in a neighborhood rife with drug use. "By being able to provide these services on site," says Flynn, "we are prepared in the event of an emergency, and we don't have to send the women out and run the risk of losing them. At county hospitals you can wait hours and hours for medical care, so the on-site medical treatment has been critical."

The program offers classes leading to a high school equivalency diploma, help in acquiring job skills and a job, and help in choosing peers who are not in the drug culture. While in treatment, clients are given business passes to leave the institution to apply for public aid and housing and to take care of other needs. When asked how she defines and measures success, Flynn says,

One of the criteria is the delivery of a drug-free baby; another criterion is the mom staying in the program throughout the whole pregnancy. I look at any type of recovery time as success. But I think that true success would be indicated by a mother who has developed a solid after-care plan for living in safe, affordable housing, understanding what the needs of her children are, and understanding what her own needs are in order to maintain her sobriety. This includes attending twelve-step meetings, which means maintaining and further developing a support system.

To leave the center with her baby, a mother is required to have a solid structure waiting for her. If she is a full-time mother, she is viewed as successful as long as she does not become too isolated. The ideal is to have a support system in place. Success after release from the program is more likely if the mother has a support system and a solid after-care plan. For Flynn, these predict success and recovery:

We ask that the client get together a preliminary after-care plan and go over that with the counselor. The counselor can give feedback as to the feasibility of the plan. The program offers a continuum of care through the Merryville Program, conducted jointly with Merryville Academy, a large child welfare agency. Once a mother delivers, if she is assessed to still need treatment and education related to parenting skill development, she can move over into the "postpart" program and continue in treatment with her infant. Merryville has alumnae nights, when the client can come back and participate in one of the self-help groups to maintain the support they developed while in treatment.

What makes the Haymarket Center program unique is that it treats its clients in a centralized, multiservice complex. Everything—prenatal care, postpartum treatment, and a recovery home for those still battling their addictions after delivery—takes place at the center. Thus the center is involved with the client from initial intake to the postbirth stages, all the while paving the way for the reintegration of the mother into society. A great deal of ingenuity and resourcefulness is required on the part of the staff to ensure that a client does not fall through the cracks once she leaves Haymarket.

Those clients who do not enter the program until the seventh or eighth month of their pregnancies are faced with critical decisions. They must decide how to ensure that they will deliver a healthy baby and how to organize their postdelivery lives to ensure that they can keep their children. The most serious problem they face is one of time, because their short stay in the Maternal Addiction Program will not be long enough to resolve their many problems before delivery. In these cases, women are allowed to stay on as postpartum clients with their infants until they are ready to return to the outside. They are allowed to continue treatment and to work on the issues that arise during the postpartum period. "This can be an incredibly vulnerable time for clients that are new in recovery," says Flynn. "I think that that support needs to continue to be there."

The program has a year-to-year contract with the Illinois Department of Human Services' Office of Alcoholism and Substance Abuse. Although this contract depends on legislative appropriations, funding cuts are unlikely because Illinois has made pregnant addicts a priority. The uncertainties brought on by welfare reform can have adverse consequences for the postpartum population who are unemployed and who risk losing government benefits, and so the Haymarket Center works closely with other agencies to line up education and employment opportunities for its clients.

In sum, the Haymarket approach enables staff members to work with the total range of client needs, including health, education, employment, housing, and social supports. This reduces the chances that the prior problems of addiction will reemerge. Long-term involvement with clients is essential; time is needed to assist clients to overcome the barriers that can undermine their continued improvement. The program's structure has defined objectives and timetables as well as built-in support at each stage. A system of rewards for adhering to the rules increases the likelihood for success. The reassimilation of the individual into conventional society is a major goal. Success is defined as a woman who no longer uses drugs, delivers a drug-free baby, and has a strong support group system waiting for her when she leaves the center. The greatest indication of the program's success is that it has never lost an infant to its mother's addiction.

The Garden Project

Catherine Sneed enrolls recently released inmates from the San Francisco County's Jail No. 3 in San Bruno (about 125 at any given time) in the gardening project she founded about a decade ago.[4] Her purpose is to teach life lessons through organic gardening, with the objective of reducing the recidivism rate among these ex-prisoners. Those with drug problems see how well plants grow without chemicals; the more successful participants eventually make the connection between their own chemical dependency and chemical-free plants. Many of these former prisoners have survived on junk food for years, and as drug addicts have had very poor health habits. They see plants flourish with the proper nutrients and discover, sometimes for the first time, the taste of fresh food (Sneed makes her workers a lunch of fresh vegetables from the garden). Gardening provides these former convicts with several additional benefits: the ability to make plants grow; a sense of ownership; wages (they make $6 an hour); and access to other social services, including housing and permanent jobs with facilities that purchase their produce.

The basic tenet of the Garden Project is to nurture these individuals and help them overcome their problems so they can reenter society. Sneed began the project when she noticed that prison inmates typically have poor diets, that they have few or no positive role models, and that they have little or no link to the earth. Growing their own food allows them to experience a successful endeavor and to work with others in the context of the natural environment. It is thought that gardening and human growth and development are intertwined: as the inmates nurture their plants, they internalize this process, enabling them to heal some of their own social and psychological illnesses. That the project works is evidenced by the low recidivism rate among participants: it is only 24 percent for them, compared to nearly 55 percent for the average ex-offender population.

Sneed, one of "about a dozen children of a career military father and homemaker mother," was taught the fundamentals of gardening by her father. About twenty years ago, while working as a counselor in a sheriff's office, a serious illness led her to an interest in rehabilitation and the idea of taking the sheriff's prisoners out of jail and into a garden. A local merchant gave her half an acre of land in the Hunter's Point section of San Francisco, and she and her helpers put in a garden of herbs, lettuce, arugula, radishes, chives, kale, beets, and spinach. Sneed had many critics, especially among long-time staff. However, the sheriff supported her.

Thousands of former inmates have now participated in Sneed's Garden Project. The requirements for participants are that they come to work, that they work sixteen hours a week, that they earn a high school diploma if they do not have one, that they be accountable for their actions, and that they report any behavior of their fellow gardeners that might have an adverse effect on their rehabilitation. In return, the ex-offenders receive, in addition to their wages and the psychological benefits of working in a garden, help with finding and qualifying for housing, social services, counseling, twelve-step programs, and the like. There is a long waiting list of offenders who want to get into the program because of its success.

One typical participant is a young Hispanic man who immigrated to San Francisco from Mexico, had very little education, and had been involved in gang activity since he was a young adolescent. He was very hard to reach, but slowly he came to trust Sneed and worked very hard in the project. He received his high school equivalency diploma and has stayed clear of trouble for a long time. "It looks like he is going to make it," she says. Sneed describes another case that was a lot more difficult: a woman in her thirties who had run a large drug operation. "She was very tough," Sneed says, "one of the most hardened female criminals I have dealt with, and almost impossible to reach." Sneed established rapport with her when she dealt with her as a mother concerned for her children's well-being. The woman needed to see that the Garden Project would benefit her and her children. Eventually, she became an exemplary participant and now owns her own business, helps to train other Garden Project participants, and has stayed out of trouble since her release.

The Garden Project has achieved national recognition as an exemplary rehabilitation program. The U.S. Department of Agriculture, for example, recognizes it as one of the most successful crime prevention projects in the country, and environmentalists praise her program for teaching ex-offenders to appreciate the environment. Sneed's skills are multidimensional: she teaches ex-offenders how to avoid returning to jail; she teaches them job skills; she offers them employment; and she helps them find jobs and housing.

Despite her success in rehabilitating ex-inmate drug addicts and drug sellers, Sneed says she never expects participants to "go straight immediately upon entering the project. Each case is unique and presents its own challenges. She expects participants in the project to falter, because they have so many pressures not to conform. It takes time, strength, resources, and supportive people for Garden Project participants to learn the self-corrective behavior that can keep them on course, allowing them to go straight, to take care of their own needs, and to live productive lives." Sneed's goal is to help each participant achieve fundamental and long-lasting change and become law-abiding citizens living within the bounds of society. Individual successes, given enough of them, translate into systemic social change, with the potential to lower drug addiction and possession rates in San Francisco.

Catherine Sneed and the Garden Project have been the subject of media stories, and many people have visited the Garden Project to observe her work and to try to replicate it elsewhere. However, Sneed cautions that a project like hers requires long-term commitment and support. Her support comes in part from the U.S. Department of Agriculture, which has written a curriculum guide for her program. However, most support comes from San Francisco companies and private foundations. In addition, the project generates funds from the sale of fresh fruit and vegetables to some of San Francisco's best restaurants and directly to the public through its own local market. Its market is another rehabilitation tool: Sneed sees it as a way to train participants to interact with the public and become aware of different life-styles. Most notably, this public forum has put a "human face" on elderly customers who formerly might have been viewed by ex-offenders only as victims.

Conclusion

This chapter explores the way four new urban leaders success-
fully address difficult inner-city problems. The challenges they
face are so staggering that, no matter how strong their dedica-
tion, they reach only a very small number of those who need
help. They understand these limitations and also the need for
long-term commitment. They also understand that it is impossible to save every one of their charges.

They have other characteristics in common, as well. Each of
them early on established clear, mandatory guidelines, policies,
and procedures, with set consequences for violators. All of
these leaders take a holistic approach to their clients, working
with the individual within the context of the family and the
community. These leaders also play a critical role in their
organizations in training others to do their jobs well, to function as members of a team, and to make personal commitments
to excellence. They communicate well. They make efficient use
of their resources. And perhaps most important of all, their
goal is always the self-empowerment of their charges.

CHAPTER EIGHT

LOOKING TO THE FUTURE

The new urban leaders face a number of challenges as their organizations age and as they themselves must think of retiring from center stage. To carry on their work into the future, a number of issues must be addressed.

Broadening the Focus

It is important that stakeholders—civic leaders, government, business, educators, labor, faith-based institutions, nonprofits, foundations, philanthropists, and residents—invest in the long-term, incremental, durable change initiated by urban leaders. For example, a focus on early childhood development may require a broad spectrum of developmental services and protections: early childhood education, developmental day care, improved public schools, access to higher education to obtain marketable skills and to health care, affordable housing, jobs, and more. Complex problems require long-term comprehensive solutions. The residual, or stopgap, method does little more than mask problems, rarely making it possible to address the root causes.

The city of Portland, Oregon, is a pioneer in forging a cooperative approach in which government, its supportive agencies, private nonprofit organizations, and other entities serving the community combine and coordinate their efforts to ameliorate the problems of an increasingly needy population. The diffusion of programs such as the Portland model is crucial to efficiently solving community problems.

Boston's Ten-Point Coalition has exported its practices to several cities. The Ten-Point Coalition in Indianapolis hopes to save children from violence, improve their literacy, and provide inner-city employment opportunities. In Lexington, Kentucky, the coalition has two goals: to keep young people from getting into trouble in the first place and to keep predators from endangering law-abiding residents of poor neighborhoods.[1]

Walter Stafford cites New York City's religious federations—the Catholic Federation, the Jewish Federation, and the recently organized Hispanic Federation—as examples of the way groups can combine their resources to have a stronger presence.[2] Stafford, who has conducted a study of African American civil societies in New York City, notes that there is no African American Federation in New York City, although the elements to organize one exist. Benefits of federating are sharing funding, connecting service providers with those needing services, pooling information and other resources, and working on a mutual agenda.

Passing the Mantle

Building intergenerational organizations, which nurture new leadership, must be a priority for the new urban leaders. A majority of the urban leaders share a concern for and a commitment to what human development specialists refer to as "generativity"—ensuring that the next generation will be prepared for their future roles.[3] The new urban leaders are concerned with producing another generation of leaders because they understand how critical it is that their work be continued when they are no longer involved. As a practical matter, they know that it is highly unlikely that the problems to which they are devoting their lives will be solved by the time they retire.

For example, Mary Nelson, head of Bethel New Life in Chicago, has structured leadership training classes and programs.[4] Nelson and her staff recruit neighborhood leaders from local churches and clubs and the police beat. Recruits attend twice-monthly classes on urban leadership and participate in small groups that write proposals for community-based projects. Each group is given $500 to implement its project. Two-thirds of the projects involve work with children, which provides an additional opportunity to identify and cultivate the leadership skills of young people. Bethel New Life hires its personnel from the community, a practice that creates a pool of local individuals who can manage programs.

The National Black Child Development Institute makes a concerted effort to develop generative leadership. Founded in the late 1960s, the institute realized that its future effectiveness depended heavily on its ability to engage young professionals in its mission and day-to-day activities. Evelyn Moore, the institute's president, says that the institute embarked on its succession planning strategy by appointing a thirty-two-year-old as chairman of its board of directors.[5] The institute's strategy is an exemplary model for ensuring that nonprofits structure succession plans, from the governance level to staff positions.

The experience of Eva Thorne, a member of the Azusa Christian Community in Boston, points to the need for the constant modification and reevaluation of solutions as times change and as new populations enter a program. Compared to the gang members whom the community worked with a decade ago, the newer gang members it works with today are more violent, more alienated, and less fearful of the consequences of their behavior than the older members.

The See Forever Foundation

David Domenici and James Forman are stellar examples of the next generation of new urban leaders. The sons of prominent public servants, they are the founders of the See Forever Foundation, a comprehensive youth development organization in Washington, D.C., whose dual mission is to provide education and part-time jobs that teach marketable skills to at-risk, court-remanded youth. They see their work in the public sector as essentially attending to the unfinished business of their parents' generation.

David Domenici is the son of U.S. Senator Pete Domenici; James Forman, of former southern civil rights activists James Forman and Constancia "Dinky" Romilly. In 1995 Domenici and Forman, introduced by mutual best friends, established Project Soar, the precursor to the See Forever Foundation. Domenici, trained as a lawyer, had previously worked in investment banking and as a middle school teacher. Forman, a former U.S. Supreme Court Clerk, was a public defender in the District of Columbia.

As a public defender, Forman came to realize that the young people entering the criminal justice system were systematically denied viable options to better lives. Most of the juvenile offenders he defended were barely literate; many had committed petty theft or been drug runners. He termed them "the poorest of the poor," children of the underclass whose lives were untouched by affirmative action and efforts toward racial equality.

Their mutual interest in helping these young people led Domenici and Forman to launch Project Soar, an after-school tutorial and pizza delivery business. Project Soar addressed these young people's key concerns: education and the acquisition of both income and marketable job skills. Participants were recruited in two ways: Forman asked friends and colleagues to recommend young people who failed in traditional school settings but were motivated to succeed; and he brokered a deal with the juvenile courts to remand youths to Project Soar rather than reformatory school.

Although Project Soar quickly became successful, Domenici and Forman realized that they had only scratched the surface of this problem. The students' potential and needs were far greater than Project Soar could meet. Thus in 1997 Domenici became the director of the newly created nonprofit foundation, See Forever. Forman left the public defender's office to devote himself full time to launch what would become one of the nation's unique entrepreneurial nonprofits.

The See Forever Foundation has three primary components:

—The Maya Angelou Public Charter School, which enrolls seventy students in grades nine through twelve.

—The Student Technology Center, where students teach computer skills to community residents, design websites, and repair computers.

—Untouchable Taste Catering, a student-staffed business that boasts law firms and major professional associations among its clientele and that will shortly unveil a full-service wedding package.

Students are required to work part time, ten hours a week, in the two businesses.

The philosophy of See Forever is one of aggressive entrepreneurship coupled with the rehabilitation of high-risk youth in a compassionate, yet demanding environment. Personnel may be viewed as "compassionate technocrats," possessing knowledge in a variety of professional fields, including law, technology, and business.

Although See Forever is relatively young, it demonstrates an entrepreneurial focus in its aggressive, multifront expansion. Its operating budget is $1.4 million, an endowment has been established, and a capital campaign was launched to acquire and renovate its five-story building. The $1.4 million operating budget is derived from public sources (70 percent), corporations, and the private sector. The Maya Angelou Public Charter School receives $7,000 per pupil from the Washington, D.C., public school system. The school system provides some additional funding for special education and residential placement.

National media attention has been a key contributing factor in the fund-raising success of See Forever. One of the largest financial gifts came from an unsolicited donor who saw a television feature on See Forever: Donald Davis, chair and chief executive officer of Stanley Works, gave $150,000 on a one-to-one match. Additionally, local foundations are a mainstay of support. However, competition for scarce resources has See

Forever officials engaged continuously in identifying new public and private sector funding sources.

In-kind contributions to See Forever include the services of a hundred volunteers. The school day ends at 8:00 p.m., making it possible for highly skilled individuals to volunteer after work. This bears emphasizing because public schools could acquire larger numbers of volunteers if the hours were more flexible.

Crucial to the structure and success of the See Forever Foundation is the deliberate interweaving of the Maya Angelou School and the two student-operated businesses, the Untouchable Taste Caterers and the Student Technology Shop. Together, they form an inclusive and interdependent organization that fosters growth among the students. Teamwork, hard work, and adherence to strict regulations are mandatory.

The high expectations and strict rules that govern the students' schoolwork and lives promote an interdependent view of their immediate environment that imitates how society at large functions. The ability to conform to and accept the school's requirements and penalties is a critical element of the entrepreneurial, character-building process and teaches the students anticipatory socialization. For example, when students fulfill their work requirement, they are learning how to manage in an entrepreneurial business.

They are also learning to control their money. For their work, they are paid $40 a week, twice monthly, via direct deposit. A third of this is earmarked for a savings account, which becomes a mutual fund when the student has saved $500. Failure to comply with the rules means an automatic $5 deduction from their wages. The salary encourages adherence to the rules, which effectively resocializes them to law-abiding, rather than law-breaking, behavior. The use of direct deposit provides a different perspective on the use of money. Students shift their thinking from saving money under the proverbial mattress to dealing with it less tangibly.

An innovative, entrepreneurial spirit informs all facets of See Forever's mission and activities, from reorienting students toward work and investment to placing them front and center in the two businesses. Former students, now in college, work part time for Untouchable Taste, becoming role models for current students. The student-operated Technology Shop allows the students to utilize the skills they are acquiring in running a business. It also teaches them how to work with adults (where the students are the teachers) and how to build positive relationships with the community, to which they are giving something back. They have similar experiences when working for Untouchable Taste Caterers, the most coveted job among the students.

Another example of the entrepreneurial vision of the Foundation is how it structures interaction between students and the business community. Every ten weeks, students complete a three-week paid internship at a local business, which enhances a work ethic and marketable job skills. Participating businesses have included the National Broadcasting Company, the National Institutes of Health, and the Robert F. Kennedy Memorial. Ongoing relationships between the student and the organization are encouraged, developing more stakeholders, with the hope that the student will find summer, or full-time, postcollege employment.

Conclusion

The next generation of black leaders must construct a new paradigm. It should embrace democracy, ideological pluralism, leadership development that includes women and youth, collaborative leadership, citizen participation, and institutions and organizations that reflect the values and mission beyond those of a single charismatic leader. The critical questions are how to engage young people in the decisionmaking process at the neighborhood level and how to connect the social capital of young people to the social capital of the public, private, and independent sector.

Questions remain. Are the urban leaders of the future being adequately prepared to take over the organizations that address the problems of the black underclass? Are those involved in nonprofits being trained to lead in viable organizations that will be effective in helping to tackle the problems at their source? Are these leaders using entrepreneurial methods to build and sustain their organization's missions? What role will technology play in the nonprofits of the future? What role will government play? What combination of advocacy, service, and political activity will be appropriate for the future?

NOTES

Preface

1. One focus of the investigation was to ascertain the degree to which the leaders are engaged in mentoring relationships with young people to prepare them for future leadership roles. Also, wherever possible the author interviewed the young people in the organizations and discussed with them their future leadership careers.

Chapter One

1. Joint Center for Political and Economic Studies, cited in Craig Timberg and Scott Wilson, "10 Years after Wilder: A Measure of Progress," *Washington Post,* January 17, 2000.

2. William Julius Wilson, *When Work Disappears: The World of the New Urban Poor* (Alfred A. Knopf, 1996); Ronald Walters and Robert C. Smith, *African American Leadership* (SUNY Press, 1999).

3. Howard J. Karger and David Stoesz, *American Social Welfare Policy* (Longman, 1990), p. 49.

4. Neil Gilbert and Paul Terrell, *Dimensions of Social Welfare Policy* (Needham Heights, Mass.: Allyn and Bacon, 1998), p. 31. The authors argue that these programs were part of an expanded social welfare state, although the United States continued to reject a social welfare state ideology.

5. For more on the role of the movement, see Clayborne Carson, *In Struggle: SNCC and the Black Awakening of the 1960s* (Harvard University Press, 1981); John Dittmer, *Local People: The Struggle for Civil Rights in Mississippi* (University of Illinois Press, 1995); and Doug McAdam, *Freedom Summer* (Oxford University Press, 1990).

6. The election of Kwesi Mfume to the position of president and chief executive officer of the NAACP was a major departure from the organization's leadership tradition. Mfume, who served several terms as a U.S. congressman from Baltimore, resigned his seat to accept the NAACP position. This was considered a coup for the conflict-ridden organization, which had lost credibility under its former president. The election of Julian Bond to be chair of the Board of Directors of the NAACP sent a strong signal to the general public and to the civil rights community that the organization was poised to propose a serious agenda. Bond, a civil rights activist since the early 1960s, when he served as director of communications for the Student Nonviolent Coordinating Committee, had been elected earlier to the Georgia state legislature, which refused to seat him because of his antiwar beliefs. Mfume and Bond had thus already achieved national reputations and respectability before their election to important NAACP roles.

7. The election of Hugh Price to head the Urban League was similar to that of Mfume and Bond to the NAACP because of the high esteem in which Price was held due to his previous positions in the foundation and corporate sectors. His focus on education, employment and training, and the digital divide has positioned the Urban League to be a critical party to finding solutions for inner-city residents.

8. In Washington, D.C., for example, Ethiopians dominate the parking industry, Hispanics the hotel and office building service industries, Asians the manicure industry, and Middle Easterners and Africans the taxi industry.

9. Joyce Ladner, *The Ties That Bind: Timeless Values for African American Families* (John Wiley, 1999); Donna L. Franklin, *Ensuring Inequality: The Structural Transformation of the African American Family* (Oxford University Press, 1997), pp. 182–214.

10. Walter Stafford, interview with the author, March 7, 2000.

11. Ronald W. Walters and Robert C. Smith, *African American Leadership* (SUNY Press, 1999). Notes from discussion with the author.

Chapter Two

1. Unless otherwise indicated, all of the Amos quotations are from an April 10, 1998, interview by the author. Additional sources on Kent Amos include the following: William Raspberry, "Children Who Shouldn't Go Home from School," *Washington Post*, December 14, 1994; Dorothy Gilliam, "A Whole Village for the Children," *Washington Post*, April 9, 1994; Richard Price, "Fighting Violence with 'All the Mushy Stuff,'" *USA Today*, May 9, 1994.

2. Kent Amos, comments made at the conference, Solving the Urban Crisis through Sustainable Development, Brookings, April 22, 1999.

3. Kent Amos, conversation with the author, April 6, 2001.

4. Amos has had specialists design curriculums for the after-school programs, parent education classes, and other projects.

Chapter Three

1. Robert Moses's life has been chronicled in William Heath, *The Children Bob Moses Led* (Minneapolis: Milkweed-Heath, 1995). For further reading, see also Jeffrey C. Isaac, "The Algebra Project and Democracy," *Dissent* (Winter 1999), pp. 72–79; Robert Moses and others, "The Algebra Project: Organizing in the Spirit of Ella," *Harvard Educational Review*, vol. 59, no. 4 (1989), pp. 423–43; Cynthia M. Silva and others, "The Algebra Project: Making Middle School Mathematics Count," *Journal of Negro Education*, vol. 59, no. 3 (1990), pp. 375–91; Bruce Watson, "A Freedom Summer

Activist Becomes a Math Revolutionary," *Smithsonian*, February 1, 1996, p. 114.

2. See Robert P. Moses and Charles E. Cobb Jr., *Radical Equations: Math Literacy and Civil Rights* (Beacon Press, 2001), p. 201. Also, interview with Charles E. Cobb, April 4, 2001.

3. When the Algebra Project was introduced at the King Open School in Cambridge, few students in the ninth grade took advanced-placement math examinations, and of those who did, few passed. Almost a decade later, in 1991, King students ranked second among test takers in Cambridge. Similar results have been achieved in other cities, including Louisville, Kentucky, where one school principal attributes Moses' project with doubling the number of students who took a national math achievement test and scored at or above the fiftieth percentile.

4. Moses was awarded the MacArthur Fellowship Prize in 1982 and the Heinz Award in the Human Condition in 2000.

5. Moses and Cobb, *Radical Equations: Math Literacy and Civil Rights*.

6. David Dennis, who worked with Moses in the Mississippi Civil Rights movement, left a law practice to direct the Algebra Project's southern initiative at sites in the Mississippi Delta, Arkansas, and North Carolina. He had dropped out of college to work with the Civil Rights movement and became state field director for the Congress of Racial Equality in Mississippi from 1961 to 1965. Following his work in the movement, he returned to his undergraduate education and, later, a law degree. Dennis, comments made at the conference, Solving the Urban Crisis through Sustainable Development, Brookings, April 22, 1999.

7. Ibid.

8. Moses and others, "The Algebra Project," p. 438.

Chapter Four

1. Other founders of the Ten-Point Coalition are Jeffrey Brown and Ray Hammond. More information can be found at www.yesamerica. org/htlf.html.

2. John Leland and Claudia Kalb, "Savior of the Streets," *Newsweek*, June 1, 1998, pp. 20–22.

3. Sandra Gregg, "Muddy Rivers," *horizon magazine*, on-line publication of the Enterprise Foundation, October 1999.

4. The author first met Eugene Rivers in the early 1970s when Rivers visited Howard University to meet with members of Howard's Seymour Society chapter.

5. Rivers credits C. Everett Koop with helping him find the financial support to study at the seminary. Koop, who later became U.S. Surgeon General, was then head of Children's Hospital in Philadelphia.

6. Eugene F. Rivers III, "On the Responsibility of Intellectuals in the Age of Crack," *Boston Review* (September–October, 1992), open letter; interview by author, July 24, 1998.

7. Dorothy Day, *On Pilgrimage* (William B. Erdman, 1999).

8. Comments made at the conference, Solving the Urban Crisis through Sustainable Development, Brookings, April 22, 1999.

9. In 1997 Operation Ceasefire won an Innovations in American Government award.

10. See also Joanne Grant, *Ella Baker: Freedom Bound* (John Wiley and Sons, 1998).

11. Eugene F. Rivers III, "Beyond the Nationalism of Fools: Toward an Agenda for Black Intellectuals," *Boston Review* (December 1994–January 1995).

12. Gregg, "Muddy Rivers."

13. Ibid.

14. Ibid.

Chapter Five

1. Jeffrey Brown, interview with the author, July 27, 1998. Unless otherwise indicated, all Brown quotations are from this interview.

2. See chapter 4, on Eugene Rivers, for more on the Morning Star attack.

3. James Capraro, interview by Robert Margolis, October 26, 1998.

4. Studs Turkel, *Race: How Blacks and Whites Think and Feel about the American Obsession* (New York: Anchor Books/Doubleday, 1993), pp. 126–32.

5. Freeman Hrabowski, interview by the author, November 30, 1998; also see Joan Morgan, "Reaching Out to Young Black Men," *Black Issues in Higher Education* 13, no. 16 (1996), p. 16; and the documentary film by Spike Lee, *Four Little Girls*, a reference to the four young girls who were murdered in the Sixteenth Street Baptist Church in Birmingham in 1963.

6. Freeman Hrabowski, *Beating the Odds: Raising Academically Successful African American Males* (Oxford University Press, 1998).

7. Allan Tibbles and Susan Tibbles, interview by Robert Margolis, October 6, 1998.

8. Comments made by Thomas Stewart at the conference, Solving the Urban Crisis through Sustainable Development, Brookings, April 22, 1999.

9. Hattie Dorsey, interview by the author, July 13, 1998.

Chapter Six

1. Some major problems—family violence, homelessness, welfare dependency, AIDS, poor educational skills, substance abuse—have been addressed piecemeal, through specific federal legislation. See Bruce S. Jansson, *The Reluctant Welfare State: American Social Welfare Policies—Past, Present, and Future* (Pacific Grove, Calif.: Brooks/Cole, 1997), pp. 173–79; 225–35; Louise C. Johnson and Charles L. Schwarts, *Social Welfare: A Response to Human Need* (Allyn and Bacon, 1988).

2. Best Friends was organized by Elaine Bennett, wife of former U.S. secretary of education William Bennett; a member of the board is Alma Powell, wife of U.S. secretary of state General Colin Powell.

3. For more information on Prison Fellowship Ministries, see (www.christianity.com/prisonfellowship).

4. Robert Woodson, interview by the author, June 16, 1998. Unless otherwise indicated, all Woodson quotations are from this interview.

Woodson's organization is the National Community for Neighborhood Enterprise.

5. Eva Thorne, interviews by the author, July 24, 1998, and April 5, 2001.

6. Lloyd Smith, interview by the author, June 9, 2000. Unless otherwise indicated, all Smith quotations are from this interview.

7. Thaddeus Lott, interview by the author, October 6, 1998.

8. Freeman Hrabowski III, interview by the author, September 30, 1998.

9. Pablo Eisenberg, interview by the author, June 17, 1998.

10. 12 USC 30, sec. 2901.

11. The plan was to put 500,000 unemployed youths to work in forests, parks, and rangelands. The young men to be enrolled were unemployed, between the ages of eighteen and twenty-five, and unmarried. They came from families on relief. While serving in the camps, enrollees were taught new skills to better their chances for employment.

12. Richard "Dick" Boone, interview by the author, July 8, 1998. Dick Boone has worked as a top aide to Sargent Shriver, director of the Office of Economic Opportunity, director of the Robert Kennedy Memorial, and executive director of the Field Foundation. Boone takes a long view of the racial and class disparities in poor urban communities, drawing heavily on his forty years of experience.

13. Arlene Ackerman, interview by the author, September 30, 1998. Unless otherwise indicated, all Ackerman quotations are from this interview. Ackerman currently is superintendent of the San Francisco public schools.

14. Geoffrey Canada, interview by the author, October 19, 1998. Unless otherwise indicated, all Canada quotations are from this interview.

15. Joyce A. Ladner, "The District of Columbia Financial Control Board: Reforms Made in the Public Schools and Lessons Learned," 2000.

16. Evelyn Moore, interview by the author, July 21, 1998. Unless otherwise indicated, all Moore quotations are from this interview.

17. Jeffrey Brown, interview by the author, July 27, 1998. Unless otherwise indicated, all Brown quotations are from this interview.

18. The reference is to what is popularly called the Moynihan Report, a controversial document in which the author describes the breakdown of the black family. Daniel Patrick Moynihan, *The Negro Family: The Case for National Action* (Government Printing Office, 1965).

19. Robert Woodson, *The Triumphs of Joseph: How Today's Community Healers Are Reviving Our Streets and Neighborhoods* (Free Press, 1998).

20. See ibid., chap. 1; for additional information, see the National Center for Neighborhood Enterprise's web page (www.ncne.com/woodson/index.html).

21. Woodson, *The Triumph of Joseph*, chap. 1, p. 13.

22. Jeffrey Brown, interview with the author, July 27, 1998. Unless otherwise indicated, all Brown quotations are from this interview.

23. There are 14,433 people in the Harlem Children's Zone, 86 percent African American and 12 percent Latino; 41 percent fall below the poverty level. Approximately 3,428 children under nineteen years of age live in the zone; 61 percent of them live in poverty. The unemployment rate in the zone is nearly 19 percent (www.rheedlen.org/childrenzone.html).

Chapter Seven

1. Paul Adams, interview by the author, October 12, 1998. Unless otherwise indicated, all Adams quotations are from this interview.

2. Thaddeus Lott, interview by the author, October 6, 1998. Unless otherwise indicated, all Lott quotations are from this interview. Additional sources include Tyce Palmaffy, "No Excuses," *Policy Review*, no. 87 (January– February 1998), pp. 18–23; Gail Russell Chaddock, "'No Excuses' Is the Motto at This Urban Texas Star," *Christian Science Monitor*, April 6, 1999, pp. 16–17; Melanie Markley, "Many Believe 'Your School Is as Good as Your Principal,'" *Houston Chronicle*, October 4, 1996; William Raspberry, "Classroom Riffs," *Washington Post*, June 2, 1999.

3. Susan Flynn, interview with the author, October 9, 1998. Unless otherwise indicated, all Flynn quotations are from this interview. Anthony Cole, government relations director at the Haymarket

Center, conducted the author on a tour of the facility and was also interviewed on the same date.

4. Catherine Sneed, interview with the author, October 2, 1998. Unless otherwise indicated, all Sneed quotations are from this interview.

Chapter Eight

1. Leland Kalb and Claudia Kalb, "Savior of the Streets," *Newsweek,* June 1, 1998, pp. 20–22.

2. Walter Stafford, interview by the author, March 7, 2000.

3. For a discussion of generativity, see Erik Erikson, *Childhood and Society* (New York: Norton, 1963; paperback reissue). Erikson introduced generativity as one of the eight stages of the psychosocial development of the individual, which begins at birth and ends at death. For a discussion on generativity in the sociocultural context, see Dan P. McAdams, "Personality, Modernity, and the Storied Self: A Contemporary Framework for Studying Persons," *Psychological Inquiry*, vol. 7, no. 4 (1996), pp. 295–321; and Dan P. McAdams, *The Stories We Live By: Personal Myths and the Making of the Self* (New York: Morrow, 1993).

4. Mary Nelson, interview by Robert Margolis, October 26, 1998.

5. Evelyn Moore, interview by the author, July 12, 1998.

INDEX